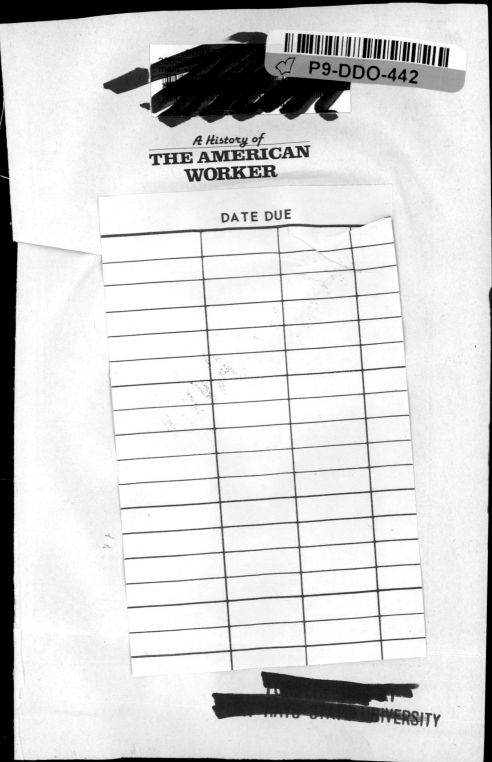

P9-DDO-442

A History of
THE AMERICAN
WORKER

DATE DUE

A History of
THE AMERICAN WORKER

Edited by
RICHARD B. MORRIS

Princeton University Press
Princeton, New Jersey

Published by Princeton University Press,
41 William Street, Princeton, New Jersey 08540
In the United Kingdom: Princeton University Press,
Guildford, Surrey
First Princeton Paperback printing, 1983
LCC 82-48564
ISBN 0-691-04697-2
ISBN 0-691-00593-1 pbk.

Printed in the United States of America by
Princeton University Press,
Princeton, New Jersey
Clothbound editions of Princeton University Press books
are printed on acid-free paper, and binding materials
are chosen for strength and durability.
Paperbacks, while satisfactory for personal collections,
are not usually suitable for library rebinding.

Reprinted by arrangement
with the U.S. Department of Labor.
This book includes all of the historical essays,
bibliography, glossary, and chronology,
originally published in *The U.S. Department of Labor
History of the American Worker* (1976), now out of print.
The picture essays and reading portfolios
are omitted from this edition.

CONTENTS

VENERATE THE PLOUGH

INTRODUCTION

It is with pleasure I note that this volume, published in the Bicentennial year, adds an important dimension to the history of the United States. It deals not with Presidents, the Congress, and the Supreme Court. Instead, it treats of the working men and women who built the nation and whose struggles and achievements deserve a central place in a people's history of the United States. This volume represents the cooperative effort of six specialists in the field of American labor history.

From the time of colonial settlement, American labor has been recruited from abroad, from Great Britain, the European continent, Africa, and in the nineteenth and twentieth centuries from Asia and Latin America as well. How labor was induced to make the long and dangerous voyage to the New World and how it fared when it first came here is the central theme of the editor's first chapter. The colonial era was the day of the handicraftsman and the field hand. To protect and advance their economic well-being, white workers—both master and apprentice, mechanic and common laborer—formed temporary combinations. The American Revolution provided an occasion for workers as well as their employers to cooperate with the merchants in protesting the new tax measure imposed by the British government. This political alliance continued down to the adoption of the Federal Constitution, which workers embraced as providing protection for their own interests against cheap labor products from abroad.

The role of labor at the beginning of the republic, in the days of Jefferson and Jackson, during the sectional conflict, and climaxing in a great Civil War, provides a cluster of themes for Edward Pessen's illuminating chapter. As the old crafts came into competition with an emerging factory system and the use of cheap, semiskilled labor, the impulse to the rise of trade unions occurred. The free labor system was marred by the exploitation of women and children, and in the South by the pervasive system of slavery, which drove free labor out of the crafts as well as agriculture. In response to new problems, workingmen's parties appeared; workers took concerted action to secure better wages and shorter hours, despite the ever-present threat of criminal conspiracy prosecution.

The third chapter by David Montgomery deals with what may well be called the takeoff point for the modern American labor movement. The age of industrial capitalism and business concentration posed severe challenges to labor to organize successfully on a national level. After Sylvis, the challenge to establish a national labor federation was taken up by Terence V. Powderly. His efforts to forge a national union of all wage earners, known as the Knights of Labor, an industrial rather than a craft organization, were tried and found wanting in the strife-torn 1880s. After 1886, Samuel Gompers, his American Federation of Labor concentrating on the crafts and stressing business unionist objectives, would hold the center of the labor stage for almost a half century. After the Civil War, instead of labor peace, one finds a series of labor-capital confrontations.

Philip Taft takes labor's story forward, recounting the continuing struggles and achievements of the labor movement from the start of the twentieth century until the Great Depression. It was a time when the federal government began to play a significant role in labor disputes, but it also marked a time when labor undertook initiatives of its own, including the arbitration machinery initiated in the cloak and suit industry. During this period the United States Supreme Court, of all three branches of the federal government, proved to be the most inimical to the labor movement.

The New Deal and World War II brought revolutionary gains for the American labor movement. As Irving Bernstein instructs us, the passage in 1933 of the National Industrial Recovery Act, which guaranteed to labor the right to bargain through representatives of its choosing—a right reiterated by the Wagner Act of 1935—bestirred labor to a frenzy of organizing; the CIO began to form industrial unions, and spectacularly successful strikes were launched against the auto and steel industries. For workers, aside from the Wagner Act, the two most important pieces of legislation in this period were the Social Security Act of 1935 and the Fair Labor Standards Act (Wages and Hours Law) of 1938.

The postwar years, which Jack Barbash sketches with broad strokes, were marked by increasing pressures on the part of management for modification of the Wagner Act, pressures which led to the passage in 1947 of the Taft-Hartley Act. It failed to choke off labor power, curtail union membership, or end strikes and work stoppages. The new antilabor legislation which federal and state governments were now enacting impelled the AFL and the CIO to put aside their philo-

sophic and jurisdictional differences and to merge in
1955 under the presidency of George Meany. To
Walter Reuther of the UAW, credit must go for his
emphasis upon health care and pension policies, while
the new AFL-CIO found such insistent problems requiring resolution as corruption, discrimination, and
jurisdictional conflict in national union affiliates. In the
1960s and '70s, as Professor Barbash has shown, the
great increase in union membership has stemmed
largely from the organization of public employees.

As a capstone to the treatment of contemporary
problems, John T. Dunlop, former Secretary of Labor,
has contributed a closing essay on the future of collective bargaining.

Richard B. Morris

A History of
THE AMERICAN
WORKER

Etching in The book of trades, or library of the useful art, *1807.*
Rare Book Division, New York Public Library.

★ 1 ★

THE EMERGENCE
OF AMERICAN LABOR

by Richard B. Morris

On August 5, 1774, just a month before the First Continental Congress convened in Philadelphia, the ship *Needham* landed in New York from Newry, England, Captain William Cunningham, master. The ship's cargo was white indentured servants. On arrival they protested to the authorities that they had been kidnapped in Ireland and had suffered "bad usage" on the voyage across the Atlantic. Whereupon the city fathers ordered them discharged. The servants had gained their freedom, but Cunningham nursed a grudge, and later, as the notorious provost marshal of the British army in America, he confined captured Patriots to atrocious prison ships and jails. The incident of the *Needham's* cargo dramatizes how the early American labor market was supplied. It also reveals that certain aspects of the old labor system were repugnant to that free society the American inhabitants sought to create for themselves.

That society was based upon farming, fishing, maritime activities, and a sprinkling of small industries. Even as late as 1789 America was a nation of farmers. The first census (1790) revealed that only 202,000 persons out of a population of 3,929,000 lived in towns of 2,500 or more persons. Recruitment of a labor force, then, was essential to satisfy the needs of farmers and to a lesser degree of the maritime trades, the furnace and workshop industries, and the highly skilled crafts.

Utilizing few if any hired hands or servants, the small family farm quickly established itself in New England, a region favoring Indian corn since it could be cultivated by hand labor, but one where diversified crops were also raised. In contrast to New England's subsistence farming, the area stretching between the Hudson and Potomac needed a somewhat larger labor force (much of it recruited from Europe) for its commercial farms, which specialized in the production of wheat and other cereals. In the South the planter soon turned to raising a specialized crop for export—tobacco in Maryland and Virginia, rice and indigo in South Carolina. The size of the plantations and the requirements for cultivating such crops necessitated a substantial labor force of both white bound labor and black slaves.

Small-scale industry required skilled and semi-skilled workers. Depending on the availability of natural resources, the colonies established glass industries, brick and tile yards, and potters' kilns; bog ores proved suitable for making castings and hollow ware, and rock ores fed furnace and forge industries. A flourishing lumber industry supported related activities such as shipbuilding and the production of naval stores and potash. New England's white pine provided masts, yards, and spars for the Royal Navy; the white oak of the Middle Colonies supplied valuable stock for the cooperage industry, and other hard woods of that area were used in the cabinetmaker's trade; in the South, yellow pine was the principal source of tar, pitch, and turpentine. Fishing and whaling required substantial fleets and thousands of sailors.

Potentially, America was a land of Eden. Labor was in demand to build homes, cultivate the earth, exploit the natural resources of the North Atlantic coast and the interior of the continent, sail the ships, and fish the seas. The colonists quickly discovered that the Indians, the native Americans who had settled the continent centuries before the Europeans, would not make compliant workers confined to settled abodes. The alternatives for labor power were to be found in the British Isles, the European continent, and along the west coast of Africa. Convinced that England was overpopulated, the government encouraged the emigration to America of the unemployed poor and vagrant class and permitted skilled workers to go to the colonies. Gradually, with England's rise to commercial and industrial primacy by the end of the seventeenth century, the official attitude changed, culminating in the enactment by Parliament in 1765 of a law forbidding the emigration of skilled workers. This was followed in turn by statutes of 1774, 1781, and 1782 forbidding the exportation of textile machinery, plans, or models. Toward the poor, the untrained, the vagrants, and the criminal class the government felt no such inhibitions; they were encouraged to emigrate to the colonies if someone, somewhere, would foot the bill for the passage.

Official obstructions notwithstanding, the importation of skilled artisans continued virtually unabated throughout the colonial years. Nor was the source confined to England. Swedes came to the Delaware, Walloons and Dutch to settle New Amsterdam. To Virginia came Polish workers for the naval stores industry, French to cultivate vineyards, Italians to set up glassworks, and Dutch to erect sawmills. Georgia recruited Italians for silk culture; emigrants from the Germanies shipped out in large numbers to become farm workers and ultimately owners, to labor in the burgeoning iron industry, and to produce naval stores. Irish flaxworkers developed the linen industry in New England as well as on Maryland's Eastern shore. The Scotch-Irish worked the far reaches of Pennsylvania and the Shenandoah Valley. In the lower South, sizable forces of Greeks, Italians, and Minorcans were transported to British-controlled East Florida.

Attracted by higher wages and the opportunity to set up an independent business or to acquire a homestead, skilled workers continued streaming into the colonies, down to the moment of war with Britain. In the postwar years, as immigration resumed, American agents scoured English towns to induce trained mechanics to emigrate in large numbers. Tench Coxe, who was Assistant Secretary of the Treasury under Alexander Hamilton, reported in 1790 that "a large proportion of the most skillful manufacturers in the United States are persons who were journeymen and in a few instances were foremen in the workshops and manufactories of Europe."

Regardless of the lures offered to working men and women to emigrate to the New World, free labor remained in short supply throughout the colonial period. As a consequence, the English settlers innovated several forms of bound labor for white Europeans and adopted a long-established coercive labor system for black Africans. One form of bound labor, indentured servitude, included all persons bound to labor for periods of years as determined either by a written agreement or by the custom of the respective colony. The bulk of indentured servants comprised contract labor. White immigrants, called redemptioners or "freewillers," in return for their passage to America bound themselves as servants for varying periods, four years being the average length of service. This amounted to a system for underwriting the transportation of prospective emigrants.

It has been estimated that the redemptioners comprised almost eighty per cent of the total British and continental immigration to America down to the coming of the Revolution. Virginia and Maryland planters who assumed transportation charges received a headright or land grant for each immigrant. In the main, though, the business was carried on by merchants specializing in the sale of servants' indentures. Recruiting agents called "Crimps" in England and "Newlanders" on the continent were employed by these merchants. They hired drummers to go through inland towns in England or along the war-devastated Rhineland areas crying the voyage to America; with the help of a piper to draw crowds, they distributed promotional literature at fairs.

On the positive side, it should be said that the redemptioner system provided the bulk of the white labor force in the colonies. On the negative side, it must be acknowledged that it was riddled with fraudulent practices and that prospective servants were lured to detention houses to be held for shipment overseas through coercive procedures which often gave rise to charges of kidnapping. The redemptioners were packed like herring in unsanitary ships; the mortality rate could run in excess of fifty percent for a typical voyage. The survivors, served inadequate rations, generally arrived in a seriously weakened condition. Once ashore, families might be broken up. Husbands and wives could be sold to different masters, and parents not infrequently were forced to sell their children. The latter could be bound out for longer terms of service than adults, even though they were shipped at half fare. Girls, ostensibly bound out for trades or housework, were at times exploited for immoral purposes.

The transportation of convicts provided another source of bound labor in the colonies. This practice, stepped up in the latter half of the seventeenth century, was spelled out by a Parliamentary act in 1718 authorizing seven-year terms of servitude for those convicted of lesser crimes and fourteen years for those guilty of offenses punishable by death. An estimated 10,000 convicts were sent from Old Bailey alone between 1717 and 1775, with double that number entering the single province of Maryland. Other convicts were shipped to Virginia and the West Indies.

Benjamin Franklin charged that the British practice of "emptying their jails into our settlements is an insult and contempt, the cruellest, that ever one people offered to another." Timothy Dwight, president of Yale, remarked that the early settlers brought with them "a collection of peasants and servants remarkable for their profligacy." Although the colonies placed prohibitive duties on imported convicts or required ship captains to give bond for their good behavior, the contractors of convicts back in England saw to it that the home government would void such laws. In the colonies, however, employers, finding the purchase of convict labor less expensive than acquiring redemptioners or slaves, were responsible for the continuation of the traffic.

The laws of the colonies added still another source to meet the large demand for labor. Persons committing larceny, a felony punishable by death in the mother country, were customarily sentenced in colonial courts to corporal punishment and multiple restitution. If unable to make restitution, the prisoner was normally bound out to service by the court. A second substantial addition to the labor market came from the practice of the courts, which penalized absentee or runaway servants by requiring them to serve as many as ten days for every day's unauthorized leave. That harsh law made no distinction whatsoever between runaway indentured servants and absentee free workers under contract, placing the wage earner and the hired laborer in the same category.

Finally, the debtor was an important source of bound labor in the American colonies. Unlike England, the colonies considered imprisonment a waste of labor. Hence, laws were enacted, releasing the debtor from prison to serve the creditor for a period of time sufficient to satisfy the debt. The Pennsylvania Council defended this practice on humane grounds, deeming it "highly reasonable that people fitt for Labour, or performing any Service by which they can earn Money, should by the same Method make Satisfaction for their just Debts."

Another method, the apprenticeship program inherited from England, had the twofold objective of supplying the labor market and providing training in a trade. The apprenticing, or binding out, could be "voluntary" by consent of parents or guardians, or involuntary, where local officials did the binding out. To get apprenticed to a highly skilled trade was a status reserved for those whose parents could pay the masters a stiff fee. Benjamin Franklin's father was unable to apprentice the lad to the cutler's trade because of the high premium demanded. Children were normally apprenticed at around fourteen years of age and bound until twenty-one.

Under the terms of apprenticeship, the master was obliged to teach the "mysteries" of the trade to the apprentice, who promised not to reveal the master's trade secrets. Colonial apprenticeship indentures generally imposed obligations upon the master considerably beyond those found in English apprenticeship articles. In addition to the common requirement of reading, writing and ciphering, colonial articles normally required the master to provide the apprentice with schooling for at least the first three years. As that paternal-filial relationship between master and apprentice gradually eroded under the emerging ethos of commercialism, masters preferred to send their apprentices to evening schools to get a general education rather than to assume that burden themselves. Other provisions, like those for clothing, were increasingly converted to money payments.

The white bound laborer dwelt in that shadowland that exists between freedom and slavery. Mobility, freedom of occupational choice, and certain personal liberties were curbed for the term of the indenture. The master had a property interest in the laborer, and except in the case of an apprentice, could sell or reassign him or her for the remainder of the term.

For black Africans a very special system of bound labor evolved. Slavery, it must be remembered, was not invented in the English colonies. For nearly two centuries before the settlement of Virginia, a trade in slaves had been carried on along the West African coast. As the English empire expanded to the New World, slave traders grabbed at the chance to make huge profits from this sordid business. Slave traffic became an integral part of a pattern of commerce, known as the "triangular trade," which operated between New England, Africa, and the West Indies or the Southern colonies. New England rum, guns, gunpowder, utensils, textiles, and food were bartered for slaves provided by West African chiefs. The human cargo was packed aboard ship, chained together by twos, with hardly any room to stand, lie, or sit down. During voyages that sometimes lasted as long as fourteen weeks, epidemics took an alarming death toll.

When the first blacks came to Virginia in 1619, they were treated as bound servants and were freed when their terms expired. In all, there were probably not more than a few hundred such cases. Sometime in the 1640s, the practice began of selling imported blacks as servants for life. In short, this form of de facto slavery preceded legalized slavery. In the 1660s and 1670s statutes in Virginia and Maryland gave slavery its formal distinguishing features, an inheritable status of servitude for life. Soon restrictions on slave mobility, along with a harsh system of discipline, were written into the "Black Codes" of all the Southern colonies.

For the South, this decision to deny blacks the status of white servants was largely grounded in prejudice based on racial difference. Those who justified slavery on the ground that growers of such plantation crops as tobacco, rice, and indigo needed a stable supply of labor ignored the fact that the need could have been supplied equally well by a system of bound servitude. Once established, the "peculiar institution," as slavery came to be called, became self-perpetuating. It was an economic system, a system of human relations, and a system of power. Southerners came to regard slavery as essential to their culture, political influence, and economic well-being.

By 1775 the stepped-up slave trade, along with a natural increase of population, had brought the total number of blacks in America to half a million. More than three-fifths lived in Virginia and the Carolinas. In South Carolina slaves comprised the majority of the population. Some colonies imposed prohibitive restrictions on the slave trade, not from humanitarian considerations but out of fear of a huge, unmanageable black population, a fear kept alive by occasional plots and alleged conspiracies. British slave traders, however, successfully pressured the home government to abrogate those duties. In the South, black slaves gradually supplanted white indentured servants as field workers. Bound white artificers were employed to train blacks in the crafts, but once slaves were trained in sufficient number, white labor became largely superfluous in slave communities. Whites who completed their terms as indentured servants in husbandry and the crafts moved to the upland regions, the bulk of them surviving as the "poor whites" of the South.

Bound laborers, white or black, received no wages. However, at the end of their term, white servants were given freedom dues, which could include clothing, a gun, and a hoe. Slaves were often allowed their own garden patches and in some cases received incentive payments for exceptional work.

Free laborers operated under a system of wage payments as today. In addition to money wages, the employment contract often included food and rum, particularly in out-of-doors trades. An alternative to wage payments was a piece-wage system. Piecework was more effective among skilled workers such as carpenters, coopers, sawyers, smiths, tanners, shoemakers, hatters, sailmakers, and weavers. Wage earners contracted for employment seasonally or annually, as in domestic service and farming; artisans were usually hired by the day or month. Collectively, these workers were called mechanics, a catchall term covering anyone who worked with his hands.

From the beginning, labor was a seller's market.

All contemporary authorities agree on the relatively high wages prevailing in the colonies. Governor John Winthrop of Massachusetts relates the story of one master who had to sell a pair of oxen to pay the employee's wages. Having done so, he informed the vorker that he could no longer afford his services.

"Sell more cattle," the worker advised.

"What shall I do when they are gone?" the master asked.

"You can serve me and get them back," was the reply.

The age-old refrain that if the high rate of wages were to continue, "the servants will be masters and the masters servants," was voiced by an entrepreneur in frontier Maine back in 1639. Samuel Sewall, noted both for his role as a judge in the Salem witchcraft trials and for his early advocacy of the abolition of slavery, sought to solve his household problem by paying court to a likely prospect. Even in the year 1687, his diary notes, it was "hard to find a good one." Help-wanted advertisements in colonial newspapers offered journeymen (free workers who worked by the day) "good," "generous," or "great wages" and "constant employ."

The labor scarcity was intensified by the lure of available land. The paradox of the high wage scale was noted by the author of *American Husbandry*, an eighteenth-century book on farm methods. "Nothing but a high price will induce men to labor at all," he asserted, "and at the same time it presently puts a conclusion to it by so soon enabling them to take a piece of waste land."

In 1767 a colonial official reported to the Board of Trade: ". . . the genius of the People in a Country where every one can have Land to work upon leads them so naturally into Agriculture, that it prevails over every other occupation. There can be no stronger Instances of this, than in the servants Imported from Europe of different Trades; as soon as the Time stipulated in their Indentures is expired, they immediately quit their Masters, and get a small tract of Land, in settling which for the first three or four years they lead miserable lives, and in the most abject Poverty; but all this is patiently bourne and submitted to with the greatest cheerfulness, the Satisfaction of being Land holders smooths every difficulty, and makes them prefer this manner of living to that comfortable subsistence which they could procure for themselves and their families by working at the Trades in which they were brought up."

Thus employers found it difficult to hold free workers to their contracts, as they would turn to farming at the first chance. French statesman Talleyrand noted this condition prevailing long after the American Revolution. He observed that as long as farming "calls to it the offspring of large families it will obtain preference over industrial labor. It requires less assiduity, it promises greater independence, it offers to the imagination at least a more advantageous prospect, it has in its favor priority of habits." Therefore, the opportunity of acquiring good land in freehold tenure was, to many immigrants, a better attraction than higher wages in the towns. This attitude pleased agrarian champions like Thomas Jefferson, who considered agriculture superior to manufacturing as a base on which to build a social and political order. "Let our workshops remain in Europe," he declared.

They didn't, of course, and neither did skilled workers. Nevertheless, there continued to be a scarcity of labor. As a result, wages throughout the colonial period stood at a considerably higher level than rates prevailing either in England or on the Continent. In 1700 an unskilled workman in England was getting 1s. 2d. a day, a craftsman 2s. In the colonies the minimum cash wage would be double that. All commentators attest to the relative lack of poverty in America in colonial times and the higher standard of living enjoyed by American workers as compared with their European contemporaries.

Needless to say, the scarcity of labor combined with prevailing high wages gave no pleasure to the employers. However, colonial governments were much more responsive to employers than to labor, and instituted various controls and approved varieties of compulsory labor. Such labor controls had evolved in England under the Tudors and even earlier. The Elizabethan statutes laid down the principle of compulsory labor for able-bodied persons in designated categories and saw to it that those living "without a calling" were compelled to work or were punished as common criminals. In the colonies labor could be impressed for a variety of public works projects, including, first and foremost, road and highway construction and repair. The inhabitants might also be impressed to work on bridges or fortifications, on repairing dams, weirs, and dikes, on clearing a commons, deepening or broadening a river's channel, and building a meeting house. The wages for such work were set by the local authorities. In the eighteenth century, workhouses were introduced in such colonial towns as Boston, New York, Philadelphia, and Charleston. Thereafter short-term labor sentences were freqeuntly imposed for minor offenses which previously had been punished by whipping.

To keep down both living costs and wages, the colonies experimented with wage and price regulation. To the transplanted English who introduced them, there was nothing new about this. Medieval statutes had fixed maximum wage scales. The Statute of Artificers of 1563 had authorized the justices of the peace to fix wages according "to the plenty or scarcity of the time."

With the English precedents in mind and the needs of employers uppermost, the colonies had a different set of priorities than Americans have today. Unlike the modern Fair Labor Standards Act, which sets minimum wages for labor, the colonies put a ceiling on wages and set a floor on hours of employment. Such regulations were initiated in Virginia and New England. While the experiments in Virginia in the 1620s were soon discontinued, the Massachusetts General Court, which almost from the beginning set maximum wages, turned wage regulation over to the towns in 1636. The Court, never explicitly abdicating its authority in this field, lamented in 1670 "the excessive dearness of labor by artificers, laborers, and servants, contrary to reason and equity, to the great prejudice of many householders and their families, and tending to their utter ruin and undoing." That body denounced the workers for spending their money on clothing which was "altogether unbecoming their place and rank" and "in taverns and alehouses where they idled away their time." Indeed, the colonial legislators supported a set of sumptuary laws which curbed conspicuous spending, denouncing expensive apparel for workers and extravagant fashions for the wealthy. In 1679 a church synod censured high wages along with Sabbath-breaking, intemperance, gaming, and "mixed dancing."

Neither laws nor church discipline could keep wages down, and wage and price fixing on a broad basis gradually disintegrated in the colonies in the eighteenth century. To have been effective, such controls would have had to be intercolonial in scope; otherwise, workers and products would move to the dearer market. By the eve of the American Revolution only the monopolistic trades—those trades which operated under a license—remained to be regulated. Authorities continued to set the fees or wages for ministers, schoolteachers, chimneysweeps, porters, and such, established the rates innkeepers could charge, and fixed the weight of a loaf of bread.

In the eighteenth century something approximating permanent labor organizations or trade unions were beginning to emerge from the industrialization of Great Britain. But in colonial America, as a general rule, the laborer procured the terms desired without having to combine with others. When American workers did take concerted action, it was invariably for a specific grievance and did not result in a permanent organization. The cases where master carpenters set up price scales for their trade are the exception. In certain trades, master workers combined to secure or maintain a monopoly of business operations and to prevent others from entering their trades, but such restraints were rapidly diminishing as the eighteenth century advanced. In the licensed trades, those who acted in concert were generally the employers. They combined with others in the same trade to secure better fees or prices, which were customarily regulated by local authority for the public interest. Today such combinations would be subject to antitrust laws.

At times bound servants went on strike, deserted, or broke the contract of employment. Such incidents were by no means uncommon in the tobacco provinces, particularly in the seventeenth century. An example of this was Bacon's Rebellion in Virginia, a broad-based uprising in 1676 to unseat an unpopular royal governor and his administration. Almost invariably such actions were ruthlessly put down by the authorities. Concerted action taken by slaves would be viewed as an insurrection, even though it might be a form of labor protest. Sporadic examples of such uprisings in New York in 1712 and 1741 and in South Carolina in 1739 were crushed with savage reprisals.

Throughout the colonies white mechanics joined forces to protest against black competition, but the problem seems to have been especially critical in Charleston, South Carolina. There, in 1744, the ship-wrights complained that they were reduced to poverty owing to black competition. Their protest, supported by white mechanics in other trades, persuaded the town authorities to enact an ordinance forbidding the inhabitants from keeping more than two slaves "to work out for hire as porters, labourers, fishermen or handicraftsmen." This resentment on the part of white mechanics was also evident in most Northern towns. But in the long run the interests of the slave-owners, not the free white mechanics, prevailed.

Strikes of white journeymen to better their working conditions, while rare and sporadic, can be found in almost all periods of colonial history, beginning with a strike among fishermen on the Maine coast in 1636. In England, following a 1731 judicial decision based on dubious precedents, strikers could be prosecuted under the common law of criminal conspiracy. However, there are few instances in the colonies where authorities challenged the right to strike. In one case the New York employing bakers went on strike in 1741 and appear to have been indicted but never brought to trial. When a number of Savannah carpenters struck in 1746, the trustees of Georgia back in England decided that an act of Parliament outlawed the action, but there seems to have been no follow-through. The experience would be different in the case of strikers in the licensed trades. Such venturesome workmen could have their licenses revoked or might even be prosecuted for contempt. But, in most cases, masters and journeymen who combined were unmolested by the law, although concerted action by white bound servants was suppressed.

In the late colonial period numerous organizations of master craftsmen sprang up, particularly among house carpenters, to fix prices and wages in the building trades. In addition, so-called "friendly" societies were organized by labor for social and philanthropic ends. In the mother country these "box clubs," as they were called, were suspected of harboring conspiratorial labor groups, but the issue was never raised in colonial America. Many of the leaders of these ostensibly philanthropic organizations were to become avid proponents of American political rights in the struggle against England.

The American Revolution diverted labor from seeking economic ends to securing more immediate political gains. In such a program workers were often allied with their employers. There was no clear employer-worker conflict evident either in the Revolution's preliminaries or during its long and intense course. While a substantial portion of the laboring class supported the Patriot cause, many workers were Loyalists. To understand why there were divisions even among working people, in what proved to be both a civil war and an anticolonial war for independence, one must recognize that there is no simple economic explanation for the American Revolution. It was not an uprising of the proletariat against a privileged class. Excluding half a million black slaves, there was not a significant segment of the population that could be considered either hopelessly deprived or condemned to poverty. On the other hand, business conditions were not highly favorable. The close of the Seven Years' War brought on a depression, culminating in unemployment and an increase in welfare payments. Commercial boycotts, initiated after the Stamp Act in 1765, the Townsend Act of 1767, and by the first Continental Congress in 1774, hit the shipping and importing trades hard. The closing of the port of Boston in 1774 created acute economic distress.

Despite the economic setbacks, there was rising prosperity in the years between 1770 and 1775. Real wages, particularly for unskilled labor, still remained far above scales prevailing either in England or Europe, and trade figures showed continuing expansion. By comparable European standards the position of the pre-Revolutionary artisan, small shopkeeper, laborer, and small farmer had definitely advanced in the course of the eighteenth century.

Numerous combinations of mechanics and laborers, masters and journeymen took concerted action in the years following the passage of the Sugar and Stamp acts. Although formed primarily for political purposes, they were in many instances motivated by economic considerations. The bulk of the mechanics and laborers were either initially involved in pre-Revolutionary agitation or were swept along in its wake and became stout Patriots. Workers in the maritime trades, for example, were recruited by affluent radical leaders like John Hancock in Boston, the Browns in Providence, and Henry Laurens in Charleston to burn customs cutters and provoke serious disturbances.

Even before the protests triggered by the Stamp Act, seamen had engaged in numerous demonstrations and riots against impressment. Captains attempting to impress seamen on the North American mainland were mobbed and on occasion even imprisoned and held on high bail pending trial. It is not surprising that a group of radical seamen and maritime workers in New York City organized as the Sons of Neptune. They apparently antedate the Sons of Liberty and may well have suggested the latter's pattern of organization. General Thomas Gage, commander of the Royal Navy in America, reported that the "insurrection" of November, 1765, in New York was participated in by "great numbers of sailors headed by captains of privateers and other ships." Shortly thereafter he referred to the sailors as "the only People who may be properly Stiled Mob," and charged that they were "entirely at the Command of the Merchants who employ them."

The leadership of the American Revolution was elitist in character. It continued to sound a strong note of legitimacy even while exploiting or condoning riots, mobs, tarring and feathering, and vigilantism. Sons of Liberty made their appearance almost simultaneously in New York and New England, but they were soon emulated in virtually every colonial town. In Boston a secret group known as the Loyal Nine (including a printer, a jeweler, two distillers, two braziers, and a master mariner—all employer mechanics) and another known as the Caucus, from which Samuel Adams soon emerged as the dominant figure, joined forces with those of Ebenezer Mackintosh and Benjamin Starr, shoemakers, and Isaac Bowman Apthorp, a leather dresser. They, along with a sizable contingent of maritime workers, demonstrated against unpopular British measures and intimidated officials who ventured to enforce them. In Charleston the mechanics' leadership allied with wealthy merchants like Christopher Gadsden. In New York prosperous merchant shippers Isaac "King" Sears, John Lamb, and Alexander McDougall kept in the forefront of radical activity; but the tasks were performed by the workers themselves—men like furniture-maker Marinus Willett, by ship carpenters, and a sizable force of seamen.

Significantly, in all three cities, the protesting merchants and shipowners formed a close working alliance with the maritime workers and seamen. Their grievances stemmed from the impressment practices of the Royal Navy. Rootless in many cases and accustomed to settling matters by brawn rather than brain, the seamen proved to be the hard core of the muscular radicals so cleverly manipulated by wealthy businessmen and shrewd lawyers.

Mechanics joined the seamen in protesting British practices. They resented the new tax measures imposed by the British government and desired a larger voice in domestic politics in order to put a checkrein on the politics of deference which governed most colonies. The mechanics, from silversmiths to laborers, were a significant force in colonial towns. According to one estimate they and their families comprised about one-half the population of Boston, Newport, New York, and Philadelphia, as well as a majority in the smaller towns. As late as 1774 the mechanics in New York cooperated with other protest groups, including the merchants. Thereafter, with the organization of the General Committee of Mechanics, they functioned independently under the leadership of sailmakers and coopers.

The demonstrations conducted by these groups transcended mere lawless rioting and assumed a moral and political dimension. They had precise targets for their vengeance and were highly disciplined. They did not commit indiscriminate arson or looting. For example, there were definite political reasons for burning the home of the Boston collector of customs Lieutenant Governor Thomas Hutchinson, detested symbol of royal authority and nepotism. Their successors, the "Mohawk braves," hurled the 342 chests of tea into Boston harbor. More disciplined than the Hutchinson rioters, they did not steal any of the detested cargo. The acts were either of a symbolic character, as with the raising of the liberty pole in New York City, or were designed to strike terror in those charged with the enforcement of the law. Mobs seized sugar and rum that had been impounded by customs officials, ventured to attack or burn revenue cutters, and pulled down the houses of a stamp collector and an obnoxious British officer who had threatened to "cram the stamps" down the people's "throats with the end of his sword." The demonstrations cannot be dismissed as mindless acts of a mischief-bent riffraff. They must be viewed as discriminating protests designed to publicize a political position or to intimidate authorities who insisted on enforcing laws deemed unconstitutional or inequitable.

Since employer and worker had a common political bond which temporarily transcended economic antagonisms, strikes were infrequent during the Revolution. However, economic grievances could trigger protests. This was perhaps best illustrated by the circumstances surrounding the Boston Massacre.

Tension was already high as a result of a series of running fights between workers in the Boston rope-walks and British privates quartered in Boston. These interlopers, who accepted low wages for spare-time employment, were bitterly resented. Sam Gray, who had engaged in a fistfight with British privates at a ropewalk, was one of those fatally shot in the so-called "massacre" of March 5, 1770. Killroy, a soldier identified as firing at the crowd, was known to have participated in the fight, as was Warren, another soldier.

The pre-Revolutionary years witnessed a number of occasions when mariners and town artificers struck in protest against British military preparations. When, in 1774, General Thomas Gage sought artificers to work on the fortifications of Boston, not only did the workers of that town refuse to work for the British officer, but New York labor fully cooperated with the striking Bostonians. Then committees of correspondence of thirteen towns adjacent to Boston adopted joint resolutions deeming as "most inveterate enemies" any inhabitant of Massachusetts or the neighboring provinces who should provide labor or materials to the British troops at Boston. Gage was forced to send to Nova Scotia for fifty carpenters and a few brick-layers, and he obtained additional workers from New Hampshire. Early in the spring of '75, mass meetings were held in New York City to protest the exportation of supplies for the use of the British garrison at Boston. The supply ship was seized by the committee and the crew forbidden to proceed on the voyage.

The relative docility of American workers in pressing their economic demands contrasted with the militancy of workers in England. Writing in 1768, Benjamin Franklin graphically described the lawless scenes prevailing in London, where coal heavers and porters attacked the homes of coal merchants, sawyers destroyed sawmills, watermen damaged private boats, and sailors would not permit ships to leave port unless their pay was raised.

When the American Revolution broke out it was reported that Great Britain had few ships for transport purposes as a result of combinations of workers and sailors demanding higher wages. Strikers slowed down or disrupted production of English firms making clothing for the British army in America; at the same time merchants were accused by the authorities of combining to raise prices of provisions for the army of occupation. Every condition seemed at hand for a coordinated attack by labor on both sides of the Atlantic against war measures of the British government. Such an alarming possibility was implied by General Gage, who reported that "the News of the Tumults and Insurrections which have happened in London and Dublin . . . is received by the Factions in America, as Events favorable to their Designs of Independency." English working-class unrest, however, never effectively grew into antiwar activism.

In the conduct of the war in America the British army employed civilian workers and also called upon enlisted men for labor services. When workers struck, the commanding generals refrained from prosecuting them for mutiny. As General John Campbell put it on the occasion of such a strike of artificers at Pensacola in 1779, such "punishment would not answer to the forwarding of the Public Works." The general agreed to overlook the strikers' "present Unmilitary Behaviour" and to forward their wage demands to Sir Henry Clinton, the British commander-in-chief. On these terms the artificers resumed work immediately. Major General Pattison, Commandant of the Garrison of New York, asserted that the existing wage scale induced no one to join the labor force: "We are now in great Want of more Artificers, but none will enter on the present Wages, and nothing prevents those we have from leaving the Service, but the Fear of being tried by Martial Law, as Deserters, which they are threatened with, in case they Abscond." And so, on the basis of expediency rather than principle, the British generals in America were forced to waive military discipline and to bargain with their workers over wages.

On the Patriot side, one of the central issues involving labor in the Revolutionary period was the control of prices and wages. When delegates from the New England states met at Providence, Rhode Island, at the close of 1776, they recommended a series of sweeping controls. At the end of January the Providence Convention's proceedings were laid before Congress with a recommendation for endorsement. In the spirited debate that ensued, radical leaders like Samuel Adams and Richard Henry Lee defended the measures as "promoting Liberty and happiness." Their opponents, capitalizing on popular objections to a revival of mercantilist controls, charged the New England states with usurping the powers of Congress. Congress did not explicitly endorse the Providence program but urged upon the other states the propriety of adopting similar measures. In fact, Congress went so far as to call a meeting of commissioners from the Middle States and the lower South. In response to this summons, a convention held at York, Pennsylvania, considered a recommendation that "the price of labor and of manufacture" be "proportionate to each other," and that prices bear the same relation to wages as they did before the conflict. Opponents of controls argued they would be "productive of the most fatal consequences." Hopelessly divided, the convention contented itself with sending copies of the proceedings to Congress and the states represented.

The failure to agree on a program did not deter delegates from holding another regional convention, this time at New Haven in 1777. Here the Northern and Middle colonies agreed on a three-zone price and wage schedule. Proponents of continued wage and price controls charged the opposition with "an idle refinement of civil rights," while their adversaries resorted to constitutional principles, insisting that any law limiting a person in the purchase or sale of his property infringed "those principles of liberty for which we are gloriously fighting."

Laboring people played a significant role in the support of Revolutionary wage and price controls. Quarter sessions courts in the respective states occasionally enforced these controls, but more often it was up to the people, organized through committees of correspondence, safety, inspection, or special town committees. These quasi-official popular groups might at times mete out rather severe punishments, such as expulsion from Patriot lines, whipping, or fines. However, they rarely used these tactics; instead, they relied upon the effectiveness of publicity. They would post in conspicuous places or publish in the newspapers the names of persons found guilty of breaches of the wage and price schedules.

It was a time when speculators and hoarders were linked in the public mind with Tories. To the populace these "monopolisers" were considered the equivalent of a "canker worm," "vermin," "rat," or "a worse enemy to the country than Burgoyne." In Boston, Joyce Junior, a working-class quasi-mythical figure, was described by Abigail Adams as leading a procession of five hundred people, "mounted on horseback, with a red coat, a white wig, and a drawn sword, with drum and fife following," bringing fear to the hearts of monopolizers and profiteers. Violent tactics were used elsewhere when public censorship did not bring about a reformation of conduct. In Philadelphia, a mob, seeking enforcement of a new price schedule and the disciplining of noncomplying merchants and financiers, attacked the residence of James Wilson, the Patriot lawyer who had defended merchants before price-control committees. A number of merchants, war speculators, and kindred souls sought refuge from the mob in Wilson's house, which was then dubbed "Fort Wilson." As one contemporary account tells it, the "labouring part of the City had become desperate from the high price of the necessaries of life." Armed with iron bars and sledge hammers, they almost succeeded in forcing the house. The mob had actually brought up a fieldpiece and placed it within firing range, when a light-horse contingent belatedly appeared.

Neither the British nor the Patriots effectively mobilized the available labor force for civilian as well as military tasks during the American Revolution. In fact, the impressment of property, particularly of supplies, provisions, and transportation facilities, was resorted to far more frequently than the impressment of labor. The Continental authorities trod gingerly so far as conscripting labor was concerned, preferring to rely upon the voluntary enlistment of mechanics and laborers in artificers companies. In Virginia the State Council refused to endorse Governor Thomas Jefferson's request that tailors and shoemakers be ordered to make shoes for soldiers. They justified their action by contending that they had "not by the Laws of this State any power to call a freeman to labor even for the public without his consent, nor a Slave without that of his Master."

For both the Continental army and the state militia it was common to advertise for forgemen, nailers, iron- and steelworkers, smiths, armorers and carpenters, and carters and wagoners, or to transfer artificers among enlisted men from regular duty to work at their own trades, with extra compensation. The working conditions, wages, and hours of laborers performing such tasks were not infrequently regulated by the military authorities. Such workmen were subject to court-martial for absenteeism or refractory conduct. Artificers in the armed services were paid lower wages than those prevailing in the open market.

"Grating comparisons" were inevitably drawn by the privates in the regiment of artificers.

Less directly the army exercised control over laborers working for contractors engaged in the production of military supplies. Contracts with private manufacturers might stipulate the rate of wages to be paid to artisans. Another method of producing military stores was by the states or Congress setting up agencies to engage in manufacturing. The most famous of these operations was the arsenal set up by the Continental authorities at Springfield, Massachusetts. Other military factories were set up in Philadelphia, Trenton, and Lancaster. To help them out, Congress or the states exempted particular workers from military service or detached regular troops for work in war-connected industries. Prisoners of war were also farmed out to war contractors, a practice the British protested as contrary to the terms of the Saratoga Convention.

Although the American Revolution was not fought for the explicit purpose of improving the lot of workers, labor was indeed a principal beneficiary of that contest. The war offered the free white male a fabulous opportunity for upward social mobility. First, he had a chance to pick up confiscated Tory lands. While those in urban areas went more immediately to Whig speculators, a good part of the rural estates of Tories was divided up according to laws recognizing tenant preemption rights. Second, there were the vast new lands wrested at the peace table, which provided veterans of the Revolution with an opportunity to secure homesteads. The new towns formed in the 1780s and 1790s were typically pioneered by war veterans and their families.

The American Revolution, which was chary about property rights of employers, did very little to mitigate or end the practice of white servitude. True, bound servants might win their freedom by enlisting in the Patriot army, but often over the vehement protest of their masters. The attitude of Patriot employers towards the Revolutionary fervor of their workers is revealed in a May, 1777, memorial by a county committee of Cumberland, Pennsylvania. It condemns the enlistment of servants without the consent of their masters on the grounds that "all apprentices and servants are the property of their masters and mistresses, and every mode of depriving such masters and mistresses of their property is a violation of the rights of mankind, contrary to the . . . Continental Congress, and an offense against the peace of the good people of this State."

The redemptioner traffic, which enjoyed boom years up to the very eve of the Revolution, came to a complete halt during the war itself. At war's end, however, it took a new lease on life, as immigration from Europe once again surged. What could be done about the redemptioner trade and other forms of debt servitude? Since imprisonment for debt was the law, with the option to the debtor of working off his debt by labor, white bondage in one form or another would survive and in periods of an economic downturn even expand. But the Declaration of Independence seems to have evoked at least one spontaneous response in this area. A New York newspaper reported that within less than a week of its adoption the state's debtors had been released from prison. That impulsive if generous action was not buttressed by liberative legislation.

So long as debt imprisonment survived, it was possible to enforce a personal contract of labor service, and its complete abolition did not take place in the states until Jackson's administration. Thus, it was not until the 1830s that one could confidently find an end to white servitude.

Freedom may have been the ultimate prospect for all white workers, but that status was not within the expectation of most blacks. Slavery darkened the Revolutionary skies as a great, brooding omnipresence. Would a revolution overtly dedicated to the principles of equality end this greatest of all inequalities? Some Southerners, like the contentious Carolina planter and ex-slave trader Henry Laurens, asserted their readiness to take positive steps. They would apply the ideals of the Declaration to the slaves on their estates in the face of opposition from "great powers," as Laurens expressed it, as well as by "the laws and customs of my country, my own and the avarice of my countrymen." Other southern Patriots, like Patrick Henry, regarded slavery as a "lamentable evil" and looked forward to the time when it would be abolished. Jefferson tried repeatedly to restrict slavery and even to bar it from all the territories, but he could not overcome sectional opposition to so drastic a social revolution. By the end of the war, slavery already was attaining the dimension of a great divisive issue. Five of the original Thirteen States, all from the North, in addition to Vermont, initiated programs of emancipation before the Federal Convention of 1787; two others followed soon thereafter. These notable actions reflected the strong antislavery impulse fostered by the American Revolution. However, even in the North the leadership seemed unable to plan effectively for the black population after emancipation, while the white laboring classes were less than receptive to the prospect of competition from skilled black workers.

These post-Revolutionary years saw the spread of the factory, the transition from custom work to wholesale order work, and the concentration of workers in certain expanding industries. In part this rationalization of industry was a tribute to tough British competition. Manufactured goods from England dumped on the American market forced employers to improvise such cost-cutting devices as increasing sharply the ratio of apprentices (now called "greenhands") to skilled journeymen and to substitute the factory for the old domestic or putting-out system. Factories required greater capital outlays than did craft shops or home manufactures. As a result, the vast majority of workers came to abandon hope of ever acquiring the means to advance into the ranks of the employer class. They now turned increasingly to the strike as the most potent economic weapon to further their interests and to the trade union as the most suitable form of organization. Typical was a three-week-long shoemakers strike in New York in 1785, followed the next year by a strike of journeymen printers of Philadelphia to protest a reduction of wages. The same year the bakers of Charleston struck to protest a City Council ordinance setting the price of bread.

Labor resorted increasingly to concerted action.

Master mechanics formed combinations of their own to deal with striking journeymen in order to secure political backing for business, especially for manufactures, and for broad philanthropic and educational ends. True, no permanent trade union can legitimately trace its founding to the years before 1789. Nonetheless, the frequency of incidents of concerted action taken by labor in the post-Revolutionary period was within a few years to be institutionalized in a permanent trade-union movement.

In each of the major American cities the mechanics emerged from the American Revolution as a significant and well-organized group. In their efforts to strengthen the federal government and to obtain protection of native manufacturers from the severe competition of British imports, labor found natural allies among the merchants. All over America a mercantile-labor alliance was formed in the Confederation years. Their supreme effort in combination was to secure the ratification of the Federal Constitution, which promised so much to each group.

In every city of the nation labor turned out en masse to celebrate the ratification of the Constitution by the required nine states. Such a celebration took place in New York City on July 23, 1788. According to a local newspaper account, some four thousand mechanics of that city representing over fifty crafts participated in a giant parade. Heading labor's delegation were some hundred masters, journeymen, and apprentice bakers carrying "the federal loaf, ten feet long, twenty-seven inches in breadth, and eight inches in height," under "a flag representing the declension of trade under the old Confederation." The blacksmiths marched, followed by the brewers, and in turn the shipowners transported a float on which rested a ship bearing the motto: "This federal ship will our commerce revive, and merchants and shipwrights and joiners shall thrive." Following, in turn, were the coopers, the carpenters, the skinners, breeches makers, and glovers, and the cartmen. The tailors climaxed the procession bearing a banner with a unity slogan: "And they sewed fig leaves together."

Under such harmonious auspices was launched the new federal ship of state. Such unity proved short-lived, however. Labor and capital would part company along political lines by the middle of the 1790s, and a series of notable strikes in the following decade would signalize the start of a trade union movement fashioned to meet the changing conditions of labor in an emerging industrial society.

Edward Hazen, Panorama of Professional Trades, 1837.
Rare Book Division, New York Public Library.

★ 2 ★

BUILDERS OF
THE YOUNG REPUBLIC

by Edward Pessen

In 1789 the British consul in America reported to London that "a series of centuries" would have to elapse before a people "possessing [so] strong a natural disposition" to agriculture as the Americans would undertake manufacturing on a large scale. His estimate proved wrong. In less than half a century the young republic emerged as a leading industrial nation, second only to England. About one out of six working Americans in 1800 were engaged in nonagricultural labor; by 1850 the proportion had risen to almost half. The second quarter of the nineteenth century saw canals, steamboats, and railroads carrying the products of American labor, opening up new markets and expanding old ones. A factory system spread from New England to New York, Pennsylvania, and the newly emerging states beyond. Banks were created by the hundreds over the next forty years. America's abundant resources, expanding territory, and growing population lured capital from both here and abroad, often spurring reckless speculation and runaway inflation.

A labor movement sprang into being in most cities, largely because workers hoped through concerted ac-

tion to maintain their earlier standard of living in the
face of rising prices. The labor movement was an urban phenomenon. Old eastern seaboard cities experienced quantum leaps in wealth and population. Western cities, abetted by the transportation revolution,
technological advance, and massive immigration, were
built overnight.

While urban life was stimulating and exciting, it
also bred social tensions and economic polarization.
And urban racial, ethnic, and religious heterogeneity
produced suspicion and discord. White workers
scorned black. Protestants of both races viewed Irish
Catholic immigrants with contempt. In Philadelphia
in the 1840s, where private fire-fighting companies
were organized along ethnic lines, native Protestant
workers often fought Irish Catholics at the scene of
fires. Bitter riots and the emergence of anti-Catholic
political parties disfigured urban life in the decades
before the Civil War.

The nation turned increasingly democratic in the
early nineteenth century. Labor benefited from the
abolition of property requirements for voting and
the increase in the number of elective, rather than
appointive, public offices. The second quarter of the
century became known as the "Era of the Common
Man" because Alexis de Tocqueville and other visitors
concluded that American democracy was ruled by
rural and urban workers of little or no property.
Labor's possession of the suffrage was a significant
achievement, unknown elsewhere in the world at that
time, yet it provided no real assurance that politicians
would devote themselves to securing labor's interests.

Labor ardently supported the Federalist party. Workers, convinced that "importations were highly unfavorable to mechanic improvement," backed the Federalist protective tariff policy. But by the end of George Washington's second term in 1796 labor increasingly aligned with the Jeffersonians. "Substantial mechanics"—many of whom were small-scale employers as well as workers—remained loyal to the Federalists, while the "middling and poorer classes" moved toward the new party. Not that the Jeffersonian Republicans were a "labor party," either in their leadership or their policies. But their antibanking, anti-British, and pro-French Revolution policies won the support of many, particularly hatters, tanners, and other craftsmen who felt in need of protection against British manufacturers. The Jeffersonians, sympathetic to newer immigrants, attracted the support of Irish and French newcomers. By 1800 most people who worked with their hands preferred the party of Jefferson and James Madison to the party of Washington and Alexander Hamilton.

At the turn of the nineteenth century, workers were differentiated by skill, income, type of workplace, living conditions, property ownership, freedom as against servitude, and relative opportunities for advance. Most were not paid in wages but in goods, crops, meals, and free living quarters as well as money. Nor were such forms of payment confined to rural communities. In the textile mills of New England, weavers typically received only about a quarter of their reward in cash, with the rest of their payment in yarn or storegoods.

The unskilled fared poorly. Laborers, canal and railroad workers, stevedores, and seamstresses, who constituted perhaps forty percent of the urban working class, received one dollar or less per day at the turn of the century. Statistical evidence for Philadelphia and other cities indicates that these rates remained stable over the next three decades. Seamen received similar money wages at the start of the period but only about half as much thirty years later.

While the dollar of 1800 was worth at least seven or eight times our own, the wages of unskilled labor were too low to maintain even a minimal standard of decent living. Price rises only aggravated the problem. According to a New York City physician, the laboring poor in the 1790s lived in "little decayed wooden huts" inhabited by several families, dismal abodes set on muddy alleys and permeated by the stench from "putrefying excrement."

Skilled workers—variously known as craftsmen, artisans, or mechanics—received from seventy-five to one hundred percent higher wages than the unskilled. Some skilled artisans owned homes, modest dwellings to be sure, yet sufficient to contain work area, kitchen, living quarters for the family and in some cases for servants or apprentices.

The tools they owned and their proficiency in using them gave skilled workers marketable assets which enhanced their sense of worth. Working independently or with others as journeymen in small shops directed by master craftsmen, they could realistically anticipate becoming masters someday. In the fashion of the time, a master craftsman supervised the production of goods for a custom or "bespoke" market.

T. J. was not president in 1810.

In 1810 President Thomas Jefferson's Secretary of the Treasury, Albert Gallatin, reported that "by far the greater part of goods made of cotton, flax, or wool are manufactured in private families, mostly for their own use, and partly for sale." Gallatin estimated that "about two-thirds of the clothing . . . worn and used by the inhabitants of the United States who do not reside in cities, is the product of family manufactures." At the time of his report more than ninety percent of the population did not reside in cities.

A contemporary account describes the extent to which the system of home manufacture had penetrated Ridgefield, Connecticut, a "typical New England town" of about 200 farm families. Few products were bought outside the home by Ridgefield's inhabitants. They made their own soap and candles as well as carpets and linen. Slaughtering was done by a butcher who went from house to house. Tanners, tailors, weavers, and shoemakers were also itinerant craftsmen. Thus, "upon due notice the circulating shoemaker came with his bench, lapstone, and awl, converted some room into a shop until the house was duly shod, the leather used being that sent back from the tanner from the hides of the cows and calves that the family had killed for meat." Hats and furniture were characteristically made by craftsmen in their own shops, often in exchange for the raw material required in their crafts. The system continued throughout the period ending in the Civil War, but by 1830 it had lost most of its vitality, weakened by the urban and transportation revolutions.

Organizations of skilled workers began to emerge in northeastern cities, particularly among printers, carpenters, and shoemakers or "cordwainers" as they were ther called. Some of these groups were confined to masters or employers, charging a high initiation fee and stiff dues that clearly priced out all but employers from their benefits. Journeymen's organizations at first followed similar practices.

These were not so much trade unions in the modern sense as benevolent organizations. The pioneer historian of American labor, John R. Commons, described both the masters' and the journeymen's associations of the Jefferson era as "mutual aid societies." They were concerned with providing death benefits to widows, assisting members who were ill or unemployed, offering loans and credits, maintaining libraries, perpetuating high standards of craftsmanship, and settling disputes among members. Some journeymen's societies had objectives that went beyond "benevolence," prefiguring the spirit of trade unionism that was to sweep across the country a generation later. Journeymen cordwainers in New York and printers in Philadelphia appear to have organized, not simply to provide themselves fraternal benefits but because they had lost faith in their old dream of becoming masters. Increasingly journeymen realized that they were likely to remain journeymen in the future. Spokesmen for the Journeymen Cordwainers Society of Philadelphia contended that they organized in 1794 in self-defense against the masters, whose own society organized five years earlier was allegedly "a league to reduce the wages of their journeymen." Increasingly journeymen's societies supplemented broad mutual aid programs with the down-to-earth economic demands of wage workers.

They insisted on a minimum wage, either a flat rate per day's work or a minimum rate for each task or piece of work completed, and demanded the equivalent of a closed shop (the term was not then in usage). Organized journeymen compelled employers to hire and retain society members only, and insisted that outsiders be made to join if they hoped to work. Nonsociety journeymen were held in scorn as "scabs." A Philadelphia cordwainer, during a court trial in 1806, defined a scab as "a shelter for lice!"

The growing militancy of skilled workers was demonstrated by "turn-outs" as they were called. These early strikes typically lasted from several hours to several days and were unorganized. The "organized" strikes conducted by the journeymen's societies were usually peaceful. But not always. In an 1806 turn-out that led to a suit against the Philadelphia cordwainers, scabs were beaten and employers intimidated by demonstrations and the breaking of windows. That strike was called to uphold the closed shop. Most strikes of the time, however, demanded higher wages. In 1791, in the first recorded strike in the building trades, journeymen carpenters protested against wages "which are, and have been for a long time too low [and] are meanly attempted to be reduced to a still lower ebb." They demanded additional pay for overtime work and a reduction in working hours.

The working day in urban shops paralleled the traditional working day on American farms—sunup to sundown. The carpenters complained that they had "heretofore been obliged to toil through the course of the longest summer's day," swearing "by the sacred ties of honour" that in the "future a day's work amongst us shall be deemed to commence at 6 o'clock in the morning and terminate at 6 in the evening of each day." The ten- or even eleven-hour working day, however, was an idea whose time had not yet come.

The right of journeymen to organize and strike did not go uncontested. Commencing in Philadelphia in 1806 and continuing there and in other cities, journeymen were hauled into court about two dozen times during the first half of the nineteenth century. Employers, merchants, and their friends—more often than not, staunch Federalists—resisted what they called "coercive" and "artificial" interference with the natural operations of the free market. In other words, they opposed wage increases. United action by skilled artisans, said one judge, is "pregnant with public mischief and private injury." Strikes, if successful, supposedly would not only harm employers but would jeopardize the welfare of the entire community. A closed shop, according to its critics, was an intolerable interference with the freedom of artisans who chose not to join journeymen's societies.

The legal weapon with which employers challenged organized journeymen was the old English doctrine of conspiracy. English courts treated labor combinations as illegal conspiracies largely on the basis of what Richard B. Morris has called an "ambiguous statement founded on precedents of dubious value," published in 1716, to the effect that "all confederacies whatsoever, wrongfully to prejudice a third person are highly criminal at common law." Employers, their attorneys, and judges and juries in America usually agreed that strikes by journeymen's societies were therefore illegal. Although English common law had no formal standing here, prosecuting lawyers spiced their arguments with references to English precedents. Defense attorneys retaliated, as in the 1806 trial of the cordwainers, when they demanded, "Where is the evidence of this common law? Is it founded on practice or usage? None can be proved! Is it founded on any legal decision? None can be produced!" And four years later, the Republican lawyer, William Sampson, arguing in behalf of the embattled New York City cordwainers, ridiculed reliance on nonapplicable English precedents, asking, "How long shall this superstitious idolatry endure?"

To judge from the actions of most juries, the appeal to English common law continued to have force in the United States. Relatively mild punishments were meted out in labor conspiracy trials. The Philadelphia cordwainers were in 1806 fined eight dollars each and the costs of the suit. Nine years later Pittsburgh journeymen, found guilty of "unlawful conspiracy" for "unjustly and iniquitously raising the price of their wages" and "corruptly conspiring" not to work for any person "who had in his employment any journeyman who did not belong to their said society," were fined one dollar each and costs. In an 1809 case involving a general strike called by the Journeymen Cordwainers Society of Baltimore only one defendant out of thirty-nine was found guilty, and there is no record that the judge imposed a sentence.

A decision by Judge DeWitt Clinton in 1810 initiated a trend toward narrowing or limiting the application of the English conspiracy doctrine. In the case of New York journeymen, Clinton described the alleged conspirators as "members useful in the community" who had erred not willfully but out of a mistaken view of the law. He assured journeymen that they had the "right to meet and regulate their concerns, and to ask for [higher] wages, and to work or to refuse to work." All that was required of them in pursuit of these ends was that "the means they used [not be] too arbitrary and coercive," as ostensibly they were in the case before him. The fine of one dollar each and costs, he assured the defendants, was meant as admonition rather than punishment. "Shall all others, except only the industrious mechanics, be allowed to meet and plot and yet these poor men be indicted for combining against starvation?" the defense had asked. Increasingly, courts and juries answered in the negative, while continuing to insist that journeymen confine themselves to "noncoercive" practices. Until 1842, courts commonly held that journeymen's unions and strikes were precisely such condemned behavior.

The technological, economic, and social changes that overtook the United States early in the nineteenth century had a marked impact on American workers. Improvements in turnpikes or toll roads gave way to a "canal fever," accompanied and followed by the appearance of steamboats and, in the 1830s and 1840s, railroads. The resulting sharp reduction in transportation costs enabled sellers to compete successfully in distant markets, opening up great profit-making opportunities to efficient large-scale manufacturers. Limited custom order and local trade gave way to a massive national market, inevitably affecting the conditions of the workers who produced for this market. It became easier, for example, to break a strike: In 1833 newspapers in Philadelphia ran advertisements for 200 workers to replace cordwainers striking in New Brunswick.

Merchant capitalists increasingly assumed control not only over the sale of goods but over their production. Their possession of substantial capital and easy access to credit enabled them to contract for massive orders all over the country. The size of their operations enabled them to cut prices below those fixed by masters and journeymen whose shops were in effect taken over by the capitalists.

On the surface little seemed to have changed. In the typical shop the master was still the chief, and the craftsmen he presided over still owned their tools. Their style of work in many cases differed little from what it had been in the eighteenth century. But the merchant capitalist supplied the raw materials and owned and marketed the finished product made in the shop. In Commons's words, the "masters now became small contractors employed by the merchant capitalist and, in turn, employing one to a dozen journeymen." Since the profits of masters came "solely out of wages and work," they sought to "lessen dependence on skill and to increase speed of output. They played the less skilled against the most skilled . . . and reduced wages while enhancing exertion."

To increase profits, masters introduced the "sweating system," demanding greater productivity from skilled workers. By resorting to cheaper labor—prisoners, women, children, the unskilled—the apprentice system broke down as employers placed decreasing reliance on skill. In printing, as in other trades, control passed from the profession itself into the hands of outsiders. As labor historian Norman Ware observed, the employment of "two-thirders" or partially trained journeymen and children reduced the status of printers from "men with a profession to wage-earners." A mechanics' newspaper complained that "the capitalists have taken to bossing all the mechanical trades, while the practical mechanic has become a journeyman, subject to be discharged at every pretended 'miff' of his purse-proud employer."

The cheapest labor, however, was factory labor. Unlike urban shops employing a few skilled craftsmen using their own tools, factories employed large numbers of semiskilled and unskilled workers operating machines owned by the companies. Two distinctive types of factories emerged. The first was the Lowell or Waltham system, named after the Boston suburbs in which it flourished. Its unique feature was its reliance on a female labor force quartered in boarding houses controlled by the factory owners. The second, the Fall River system, like the factory system in England, employed children and male adults as well as women and made no special provisions for housing. This system proved to be the most durable, but the Lowell system excited more interest.

A sharp controversy arose over the conditions of work and the quality of life enjoyed by the mill girls. A contemporary admirer described the founders of the system as "those wise and patriotic men [who] foresaw and guarded against the evils of social degradation" characteristic of the English factory system, "by the erection of boarding houses [under] matrons of tried character" for a supply of "proud and respectable girls." Charles Dickens and Harriet Martineau were charmed by what they described as clean housing and well-lighted rooms, the excellent supervision given happy and healthy young women, and the attractive conditions of work they found in the mills. At a time when the system had come under much criticism, members of an investigating committee of the Massachusetts State legislature in 1845 praised the "neatness, cleanness, good lighting, comfortable temperature, and the cheerful presence of plants on the window sills" of the boarding houses, as well as the appearance of the "healthy, robust" girls who lived in them. The *Lowell Offering*, a newspaper edited by the young women themselves, gave an impression of contented workers with much leisure time for wholesome and uplifting diversions.

Other contemporaries, however, saw a very different picture. "It is enough to make one's heart ache," wrote New England labor reformer Charles Douglas, "to behold these degraded females now dragging out a life of slavery and wretchedness" in Lowell, to observe them "as they pass out of the factory—to mark their woestricken appearance." The editor of the *Boston Daily Times* wrote on July 13, 1839, that "the young girls are compelled to work in unhealthy confinement for too many hours every day . . . their food is both unhealthy and scanty . . . they are not

allowed sufficient time to eat . . . they are crowded
together in ill-ventilated apartments . . . and in consequence they become pale, feeble, and finally broken
in constitution," and in some cases, "debauched."
Some young workers complained about overcrowd-
ing, "14 hours of toil" per day, unhealthy apartments, bad air, insufficient exercise and leisure—a
regimen which hastened them "on through pain, disease, and privation, down to a premature grave." Militant journals such as the *Factory Girl's Friend* and the
Voice of Industry concurred in the indictment.

Is the truth somewhere in between? It may be helpful to think of the Lowell system—which prevailed
also in Lawrence, Chicopee, and Lancaster, Massachusetts, and many towns in Maine and New Hampshire—as having gone through several phases. The
Boston founders of the system were, of course, interested in making great profits; that is why they sought
female labor. But they also understood that to maintain the approval and respect of the larger community they would have to provide decent housing,
strict moral supervision, and relatively attractive
working conditions. Hours may have been long and
wages low, yet they doubtless appealed to young
people used to long hours of work on the family farm
for no pay whatever. According to historian Hannah
Josephson, what drew the young girls to Lowell and
other mill towns "primarily of course was the high
wages"—or what they thought were high wages.

Wages, however, were never high. Women in the
boarding house mills earned approximately $2.50 per
week in 1830, although, as a factory agent reported, it

was "almost impossible to ascertain the wages paid by his competitors to their female operatives." They typically worked more than twelve hours per day, and minor infractions such as a few minutes' lateness were punished severely. One-sided contracts gave them no power over conditions and no rewards for work. The Fall River system was even harsher.

The search for cheap factory labor inevitably led to heavy reliance on child labor. The famous mill of Almy and Brown early in the century employed one hundred children between the ages of four and ten! In the 1820s and 1830s children under sixteen constituted from one-third to one-half the labor force of New England. Their wages hovered around thirty-three cents per week, with fifty cents the average in Rhode Island. No wonder a cotton mill in that state in 1828 put up the following notice: "Wanted. Four families with not less than four children each to work in the mill." Children made up about one-fifth of the Pennsylvania labor force, averaging between seventy-five cents and two dollars per week. In that state, conditions of all factory workers deteriorated in the years before 1840. Wages declined, hours of work were lengthened, penalties were imposed for violations of "arbitrary regulations of lopsided labor contracts." Long hours typically meant more than twelve hours. In several New Hampshire factories, managers even made the clock run slow at night in order to get an extra half-hour out of the workers.

In the South the industrial sector thrived on slave labor. A Northerner visiting the antebellum South observed that slaves were "trained to every kind of manual labor. The blacksmith, cabinetmaker, carpenter, builder, wheel-right—all have one or more slaves laboring at their trades." Blacks worked as metal mechanics, machinists, shoemakers, bakers, printers, papermakers, textile workers, in every kind of processing, whether of sugar or rice, as lumber and turpentine workers, salt boilers, as steamboat deck hands, firemen, engineers, occasionally as pilots, and as bridge builders. Slavery was particularly important in the South's substantial iron industry. In the Tredegar Iron Works in Richmond, the nation's third largest iron company, slaves constituted about one-half the labor force of 1,000. They were engaged in every phase of production, whether as founders, colliers, miners, teamsters, or woodchoppers. At blast furnaces blacks were employed together with a "handful of skilled laborers, usually but not always white," under the direction of a white manager.

Some white workers bitterly resented the hiring of blacks as skilled or semiskilled mechanics. In 1847 striking white workers at the Tredegar company threatened not to return unless recently employed blacks were removed from specified furnaces and mills of the company. Their strike was unsuccessful.

White employers insisted on hiring black labor, not only for its cheapness but for its skill. A white foreman in a southern textile plant observed that blacks did "fully as much work [as whites]" and were "much more attentive to the condition of their looms." An Alabama mine owner reported that "every day's experience confirms my opinion that it is next to impossible to prosecute my mining interest successfully with free white labor. It was unruly, unreliable, and expensive." He concluded: "I must have a Negro force or give up my business." Although industrial slaves fared better than their brothers and sisters in the fields, they were subjected to hard work and long hours. In Louisiana sugar refineries, many worked an eighteen-hour day. They had to accommodate themselves to the whims of their masters and occasionally suffered the "brutality that was an integral part of bondage." The fact remains, as Morris showed, that in Virginia, skilled slaves who were hired out received wages, held property, and possessed "some measure of mobility and free choice that compared favorably with the lot of the unskilled."

Living conditions of black workers in the South, according to historian Charles B. Dew, improved modestly. Workers used their pay for "overwork" to buy goods, achieving a degree of material competence unknown to most slaves. While Dew found instances of whipping and cruelty, they were the exception. Iron men sought profit, not the joys of sadism, and treated the skilled labor upon which profit depended accordingly. Instead of degrading the workers, industrial slavery "in some ways . . . provided an environment in which they could develop some sense of personal dignity and individual initiative in spite of the psychological and physical confines of their bondage." The system functioned "more through mutual accommodation than outright oppression."

The situation of black labor in the antebellum South is better understood when viewed in the context of the situation for all labor in that section. Num-

erous whites, particularly poor laborers, were reduced
to a "bound" or semifree status. Many white seamen
in the section were treated more brutally than were
slaves. Imprisonment for debt may have been abolished in most of the North during the Jacksonian era,
but not in the South.

Workers in the early nineteenth century, whether
factory operatives or skilled mechanics, did not live
to work. They loved leisure; plant breakdowns or
delays in transporting raw materials were often regarded as offering a splendid opportunity for diversion. An "elderly tailor" in Philadelphia corrected an
onlooker's impression that the artisan and his fellows
were headed toward a field because they had been
laid off. "Not at all, we are only enjoying the Tailor's
Vacation," the worker explained. "Pressure is well
enough to be sure, as I can testify when the last dollar is about to be pressed out of me; but Vacation is
captial. It tickles one's fancy with the notion of choice.
'Nothing on compulsion' is my motto."

Workers enjoyed fun and games outside of work
and insisted on introducing them into workshop and
mill as well. Required to do compulsory militia service, many artisans turned the occasions into "scenes
of riot and disorder," scandalizing the champions of
industrial discipline who regarded them as "disgust-
ing and harmful." Philadelphia's artisans, no doubt
like those in other cities, delighted in cockfights,
roulette, circuses, shooting matches, hunting, and foot-
racing. Herbert G. Gutman has disclosed that "hunting, harvesting, wedding parties, frequent 'frolicking'
that sometimes lasted for days, and uproarious Elec-

tion and Independence Day celebrations plagued mill operators."

The modern coffeebreak is a pale replica of an old institution. After finishing a difficult job, cabinet-makers in New York City sent out an apprentice who "speedily returned laden with wine, brandy, biscuits, and cheese." In shipyards in the same city, all work ceased several times a day as "every man and boy" in the yard was supplied with "cake or crullers, doughnuts, gingerbread, turnovers, a variety of sweet cookies," and liquid refreshments.

The American worker loved to drink, insisting that liquor be brought in during working hours. That a shipbuilder in Medford, Massachusetts, who refused his men "grog privileges" managed nevertheless to have work completed on a ship has been called a remarkable achievement. Philadelphia artisans insisted on their late afternoon drink, passing a jug around. Not that they abstained earlier. A journeyman there reported that "young apprentices learned to drink while they learned a trade." The youths made periodic trips to the local pub to fill the flasks journeymen brought with them to work. Before returning to the shop the apprentice would "rob the mail"—help himself to a drink. In Lynn's shoemaking shops, historian Paul Faler has found that "no working man would labor unless his employer provided a half pint of liquor per day as part of his wages." Cordwainers drank their daily pint of "white eye," some even "going the whole quart." In the morning and afternoon an apprentice was sent out for "black stop," a concoction made of rum and molasses. The person who made the best shoe was expected to treat, while "the botch who made the worst one also paid the 'scot.'" On coming of age, a worker was expected to provide the "choicest liquors for visiting well-wishers."

To an avowed socialist like William Haighton, organizer of the Philadelphia trade union movement in 1827, drinking, "gaming and frolicking" were a snare and a delusion that workers would have been wise to put aside. Interestingly, the line that American workers should turn from intoxicating beverages and "idle pastimes" to sobriety, education, and moral discipline was advocated by labor radicals, moralistic Protestants, social conservatives, and many employers.

Ideas also intoxicated workers. Beginning in Philadelphia in 1828, a labor movement spread throughout the country during the early 1830s. It consisted of unions and political organizations known as Workingmen's parties. Historian John R. Commons described these groups as America's pioneer labor movement because, for the first time, journeymen's societies in different crafts combined to form one union of the trades—or "'trades' union" as it was then known—in most of the cities of the country. The members of these organizations generally were skilled artisans or mechanics rather than laborers or factory workers. The latter did organize from time to time but most of their attempts failed. The fear that the spread of the factory system would jeopardize the status of skilled artisans impelled many of them to unite. Another reason for organizing was that incomes, insufficient to begin with, were threatened both by inflation and employer pressure to cut wages.

Living conditions even of skilled mechanics were yet another source of irritation. Working-class housing was typically crowded, noisy, and marked by inadequate sanitation and rubbish removal. The era's urban improvements, whether in water supply, street paving, lighting, or safety, were characteristically introduced first to the quarters of the well-to-do. The streets and wards or districts of antebellum cities were clearly differentiated by wealth and class. The rich lived in elegant mansions in exclusive enclaves, leaving the mass of urban inhabitants to the "working-class wards." This pattern prevailed for old seaboard cities such as Boston, Philadelphia, and New York, and newer western cities such as Pittsburgh, Cincinnati, and Natchez. Wealth was grossly maldistributed in antebellum towns and cities. The working people who made up the majority of the urban population owned a pitifully small portion—about five percent or less—of urban wealth.

A contributor to a Philadelphia newspaper in 1831 cheerfully advised that "with few exceptions, frugal industrious journeymen, unencumbered with families, may save so much of their wages, as in a few years to be enabled to commence business on their own account." A few years later a judge in New York City, at the same time that he branded striking unions as illegal combinations that allegedly were "mainly upheld by foreigners," assured mechanics that in this "land of law and liberty, the road to advancement is open to all and the journeymen may by their skill and industry, and moral worth, soon become flourishing master mechanics" or employers. The men who flocked to the labor organizations showed their disbelief in such comforting promises.

A number of the workingmen's parties were "workingmen" in name only. Yet most of the organizations were authentic. Their memberships were typically small, but that was due in large part to the savage attacks levelled at them by a hostile press. The Boston manufacturer Amos Lawrence, snorting that "we are literally all working men," charged that "the attempt to get up a 'Working Men's party' is a libel upon the whole population, as it implies that there are among us large numbers who are not working men." A more characteristic attack on the new parties took the form of name-calling. They were denounced as "agrarians" or anarchists, "levellers," a "mob," a "rabble," the "dirty-shirt party," "tag, rag, and bobtail," and "ring-streaked speckled rabble."

The Philadelphia party arose out of a decision by the city's Mechanics' Union of Trade Associations to enter into politics in order to promote "the interests and enlightenment of the working classes." This union consisted of societies of painters, glaziers, bricklayers, typographers, and journeymen of a dozen other trades. The Philadelphia party, like so many others, was led by or nominated to office men who were themselves not workers. Stephen Simpson, political candidate of the party, was the well-to-do son of an officer in the great Girard Bank. Robert Dale Owen, a leader of the Workingmen's party in New York City, was the son of a factory owner and had known comfort, even luxury, from childhood. Simpson and Owen, embracing radical social principles that were in some respects socialistic, believed that labor created all wealth and that inequality and social distress were caused by private property.

The many dozen parties in the towns and cities of the country made no attempt to form a national organization, and each went its own way. Yet the program championed by their party journals was amazingly similar. The Philadelphia *Mechanic's Free Press*, the New York *Working Man's Advocate*, and the Indianapolis *Union and Mechanics' and Working Man's Advocate* all listed similar demands. Some of these associations called for an equal distribution of property, others for state-run boarding schools to instill new ideas in the young of the next generation. There was almost universal support for trade unions and mechanics' lien laws to assure that workers had first call on their employers' payrolls; abolition of imprisonment for debt; a tax-supported public school system free of a degrading paupers' oath requirement; reform of a militia system that permitted those able to afford it to avoid service; simplification of the legal system, as well as making it less expensive; and abolition of the system whereby state legislatures enacted special laws conferring monopolistic charters on favored bank directors and other entrepreneurs.

The Workingmen's parties were characteristically disdainful of the major parties. They might on occasion support one or another of them on a given issue, such as backing the Democratic "war" against the second Bank of the United States. In that famous affair, President Andrew Jackson and his party tried to give the impression that they opposed the rechartering of the bank because it allegedly oppressed labor and the poor. Actually, the needs and welfare of labor had nothing to do with the issue. For all his reputation as a champion of have-nots, Jackson paid little attention to labor. He was in fact the first presidential strikebreaker, sending in federal troops to crush a strike of workers against a canal company directed by his friend John Eaton.

The cornerstone of the labor movement, however, was not ephemeral political organizations but trade unions. The first trades' union—or merging of separate journeymen's societies—took place in New York City on August 14, 1833. Realizing that individual societies could not cope singlehandedly with employers, artisans all over the country quickly followed the lead of the New Yorkers. Carpenters, bakers, soap makers, printers, cabinetmakers, masons, bookbinders, house painters, combmakers, brush makers, tailors, hat makers, weavers, jewelers, blacksmiths, machinists, rope makers, sailmakers, carvers, gilders, cordwainers, chairmakers, and artisans in dozens of other occupations formed new societies or flocked to old ones. Unions sprang up in Philadelphia, Boston, Baltimore, Washington, D.C., Newark, New Brunswick, Albany, Schenectady, Pittsburgh, Louisville, Cincinnati, St. Louis, and most other urban areas.

The new unions were led by idealistic radicals, many of whom denounced private property and the wage system as the root causes of poverty and injustice. Union journals show that every variety of social, economic, political, and judicial reform attracted them and evoked their sympathy. The unions' actions, however, make clear that broad reforms were peripheral. The central interest was wages and hours, the characteristic activity the strike.

Strikes for the ten-hour day were often unsuccessful. In Boston in 1825 the journeymen house carpenters had struck against the sunup to sundown working day they found so "derogatory to the principles of justice and humanity." The master carpenters on the other hand had defended the long working day as "that which has been customary from time immemorial." Backed by merchant capitalists who denounced the strike as a nefarious scheme allegedly put forward by foreign agitators and a press controlled by these merchants, the masters and their influential allies defeated the strike. In 1832, when the house carpenters were joined by journeymen ship carpenters, masons, painters, and sailmakers from Boston and nearby suburbs, a ten-hour strike was again crushed by the powerful alliance of masters, capitalists, and press.

By the mid-1830s, however, the movement was doing better, at least outside of Boston. In Philadelphia, the achievement of the ten-hour day in 1835 was hailed by unionists as the accomplishment of labor's "bloodless revolution." The national government implemented it first in the Navy Yard in 1836 and for all public works four years later.

Workers had a sense of solidarity that at times transcended the boundaries of their union, but the era's union movement was essentially an intra-urban phenomenon. Although on occasion unionists in one city helped their beleaguered colleagues in another, the central preoccupation of the membership was with conditions in their own community. Significant attempts at creating a national organization were made not by the unions of the different cities but rather by individual crafts. Journeymen house carpenters, handloom weavers, combmakers, cordwainers, and printers took steps to create national societies that would cut across the boundaries of the city and its trades' union. The New York City union journal *The Man* claimed that the unions had 200,000 members. While most crafts in most towns and cities had societies that in turn belonged to unions, these largely successful organizations did not last long. What did them in was the depression that followed the panics of 1837 and 1839.

Labor suffered for almost a decade in some communities after the debacle of 1837. Lynn, Massachusetts, shoe workers had to forage in the woods for fuel, eat dandelions, and obtain other food by bartering with nearby farmers and fishermen. The New York *Tribune* in July, 1845, estimated that close to one-third the adult male population remained unemployed. A well-to-do Philadelphian, in a diary entry in 1842, observed that the city's streets were deserted, business was at a standstill, sheriffs' sales were commonplace, and the "injuries of poverty are felt by both rich and poor." Most unions and their member societies disappeared in a time when workers found it impossible to maintain dues payments.

Nonpayment of dues figured in the landmark decision of 1842 handed down by Lemuel Shaw, Chief Justice of the highest court of Massachusetts, in the case of *Commonwealth v. Hunt*. It turned on the

refusal of members of the Boston Journeymen Boot-
makers Society to continue working in a shop that
would employ a nonmember. In the case, suit was
brought by the nonmember, Jeremiah Horne, when
his employer at the society's behest fined Horne for
his delinquent dues payments to the union. Shaw's
decision held that "the common law in regard to conspiracy in this Commonwealth is in force," thus cater-
ing to conservative opinion's reverence for "tradition."
Shaw divided conspiracy into two parts: There had to
be either "some criminal or unlawful *purpose,* or to
accomplish some purpose, not in itself criminal or
unlawful . . . criminal or unlawful *means.*" When Shaw
declared that the society's purpose of inducing "all
those engaged in the same occupation to become members of it" was not unlawful, he provided the first
affirmative legal sanction to unionism and the closed
shop. Almost anticlimactic was his finding that the
means used to withhold labor were also not unlawful.

Unionism did not leap forward as a result of this
decision. Nor did conspiracy trials cease altogether.
Yet there can be little doubt that the legal recognition
of the rights of unions played an important part in
abetting their later growth.

Industrial production soared after the early 1840s.
In the space of five years, iron production increased by
more than 300 percent, anthracite by 1,000 percent,
and ship tonnage by about 250 percent. Although
factories expanded, relatively small shops accounted
for most of the labor force. Philadelphia's textile factories, which after the consolidation act of 1854 num-

bered 260, continued to have their weaving done by weavers working handlooms in their own homes.

In the 1850s a number of large foundry owners in Pennsylvania, eager to corner the national market, sought to destroy their competitors by a ruthless attack on the wages and conditions of skilled molders. Piecework became the rule, performed by poorly trained and poorly paid helpers and apprentices. Skilled workers were now forced to buy their own tools, purchase their necessities in company stores, waive their rights to damages for injuries suffered at work, and submit to withholding of part of their pay until work season's end as an assurance of their good behavior! As for conditions in foundries, an observer whose report appeared in the *Atlantic Monthly* described a ghastly scene of "masses of men with dull, besotted faces bent to the ground . . . begrimed with smoke and ashes, stooping all night over boiling cauldrons of metal."

A new development in the factory system in some areas was the decreasing reliance on child labor. The change was occasioned by the introduction of heavier, more difficult machinery requiring adult workers. In much of New England, these were increasingly Irish immigrants. Factory workers were not held in high regard. A foreman told a visitor to Fall River in 1855, "I regard my work people just as I regard my machinery . . . When my machines get old and useless, I reject them and get new, and these people are part of my machinery."

Evidence indicates that workers did not do well during the prosperity that ostensibly returned in the

mid-1840s. The chronically desperate plight of the unskilled, such as female needleworkers, was a function
of their wages of less than a dollar per week. Between 1837 and 1858 the wages of skilled iron workers
in Pennsylvania were reduced by one-third to one-
half. On May 27, 1851, Horace Greeley's *Tribune*
itemized a "Budget for a Family of 5 for one week."
Their expenses came to $10.37 for goods and services
that were confined to the bare necessities. For as
Greeley asked in an accompanying editorial, "Where
is the money to pay for amusement, for ice cream,
puddings, trips on Sunday . . . in order to get some
fresh air, to pay the doctor or apothecary . . . to
purchase books?" It has been estimated that at the
time, shoemakers, printers, hatters, cabinetmakers,
and most others were averaging roughly one-half the
necessary wage—a wage itself found "inadequate to
maintain the worker's family at anything like a
decent comfort standard." The head of the Journeymen
House Carpenters of Philadelphia wrote that costs of
a decent house with a bathroom, cellar, furniture,
bedding, clothing, and amusements left workers without sufficient income to adequately feed their families.

Workers were disheartened too by impersonal .rela-
tionships in shop and factory. A machinists' and blacksmiths' leader, recalling an earlier time when "every
worker knew his employer," observed that now "men
and masters became estranged and the gulf could
only be healed by a strike."

Few workers appear to have responded to the
call by some of their leaders that labor adopt one or
another variety of socialism. The National Typographi-

cal Society in 1850 attacked the wage system, urging labor to "become its own employer, to own and enjoy itself the fruits" of its work. But few workers outside the society listened. A more typical response was the strike. An "epidemic" of strikes swept over the country in the 1840s as business boomed, prices soared, and wages lagged. Some of these were staged by labor "protective associations," but many were spontaneous. Another wave of strikes in the 1850s was almost entirely organized by trade unions.

The nation's second great surge of unionism occurred at mid-century as journeymen once more combined. Influenced at first by the earlier benevolent societies which had included masters in their membership, the new unions quickly moved to oust all but wage workers. Stripped of what Commons called "universal and glowing ideals," skilled mechanics "settled down to the cold business of getting more pay for themselves." These unions concentrated on the closed shop, rules of apprenticeship, wages and methods of payment, strike and members' benefits. They published no journals, substituting strikes for grandiose proclamations. In 1853-1854 alone they staged about 400 strikes, mostly for higher wages.

These strikes did not follow negotiations as we know them. Instead, unions would decide on their objectives and then issue notices such as the following: "On Wednesday evening September 4 the Bricklayers and Plasterers by an unanimous vote declared that they would not work after Wed. the 11th inst. for a sum less than $2.00 per day, on and after that day." If the employer accepted these terms a "trade agreement" was concluded. Such agreements were sought not only from individual employers but from employers' associations, in order to establish uniform wages and other conditions in a craft. Strikes were often directed against recalcitrant or non-association employers.

Once again several unions attempted to organize nationally. The results were not very much more impressive than they had been twenty years earlier, since only three of the dozen or so national unions created in the 1850s managed to survive the depression that followed the Panic of 1857. These were the National Typographical Union, the Machinists' and Blacksmiths' International Union, and the Iron Molders' International Union. While impersonal factors, such as the maturing of a national market, obviously had much to do with the emergence of national unions, the efforts of dynamic individuals such as William Sylvis of the molders cannot be discounted.

One of the most inspirational figures in the history of the labor movement, Sylvis's experiences as a worker reflect the changes that transformed both the economy and the situation of labor in the decades before the Civil War. Sylvis's father was a wagon-maker so poor that during the post-1837 depression he had to "place" the youngster with a well-to-do family as an apprentice. On completing his five-year term, Sylvis was given the traditional "freedom suit" of broadcloth, white shirt, woollen hose, calfskin boots, and high silk hat. A leader of the molders' organization in Philadelphia, Sylvis played the decisive part in creating a national molders' union in 1859. Four years later he became the president of the organization, after journeying to shops and foundries in the United States and Canada, listening to workers' grievances, disregarding employer threats, and building the union. He lived from hand to mouth during this ordeal. Sylvis always lived on the brink of poverty, even during the years of his presidency of the international union. When he suddenly died in 1869, he only had one hundred dollars and his family could not meet the costs of burial.

Whether national or local, most unions were destroyed in the wake of the Panic of 1857. On the eve of the Civil War, spokesmen for organized labor cast their lot with the conciliators who would avoid bloodshed at almost all costs. At a workers' meeting in Louisville on December 28, 1860, friends of William Sylvis, while pledging allegiance to the Constitution and the Union, denounced the "politicians" who had allegedly brought the nation to the brink of an unnecessary war. Labor meetings early the following year were held in Newark, Reading, Harrisburg, Philadelphia, St. Louis, Cincinnati, Louisville, Norfolk, and Richmond, supporting the Crittendon Compromise, which would have legitimized slavery in the territories south of the 36°30′ line. Sylvis chaired a meeting in Philadelphia on February 22, 1861, that adopted resolutions in support of the Crittendon plan and the "equal rights of the South in the territories," while denouncing all measures likely to result in war.

The attack on Fort Sumter changed all that. Sylvis himself assisted in recruiting a volunteer company of molders, as he and most other northern leaders rallied to the cause. It has been estimated that mechanics and laborers constituted forty-two percent of the Union army, while skilled artisans were enthusiastic volunteers. Their patriotism had the effect of decimating trade union ranks. Thus one Philadelphia union closed up shop for the duration, resolving "to enlist with Uncle Sam," adjourning "until either the [Federal] Union is safe or we are whipped." Foreign-born workers as well as native-born demonstrated a devotion to the Union that, according to historian David Montgomery, was "rooted in the intense nationalism of the working class." As the war continued, some workers opposed particular governmental policies, such as emancipation or a draft which discriminated against the poor. But their general support of the Union cause did not flag: they accepted emancipation when it came and opposed the draft riots.

The war had mixed consequences for labor. Inflation and mounting taxes hurt workers. Several western states passed antistrike laws, and eastern states gave serious consideration to such measures. Nor did the national government display much sympathy for labor. Workers in the great federal workshops in Nashville were defrauded of what they believed to be their rightful wages. They were not given the promised time and a half for overtime and were deprived of part of their wages if they quit. In the Brooklyn Navy Yard the back pay of striking molders was confiscated.

Military force was used against striking workers. Leaders in the strike at the famous Parrott gun works in Cold Springs, New York, were imprisoned without trial. In Louisville, General Burbridge drove strikers back to work at the point of bayonets, while in St.

Louis General Rosecrans charged picket lines and strike meetings. Soldiers in Tioga County, Pennsylvania, arrested the striking miners' leaders, forcing the rank and file to surrender to the owners under the threat of starvation.

Strikes not only persisted, however; they multiplied swiftly. They were reactions to a sharp rise in the cost of living that was not matched by wage increases for the great army of unskilled workers.

Trade unions experienced a renaissance during the war, the number of locals increasing by 350 percent between December, 1863, and December, 1864. Unlike the movement of the previous decade, Civil War unions were most articulate, publishing many prolabor journals. These unions consisted primarily of urban artisans, some of whom—like the iron molders—spoke for the unskilled workers in their shops and factories. The trades' assemblies of different unions in a city, similar to the "Unions of the Trades" of the 1830s, was a significant development. Between 1861 and 1865 there emerged more than a dozen national unions, ranging from miners, locomotive engineers, and cigar makers to plasterers, tailors, bricklayers, and printers. Owing much to technological and commercial changes that rendered more parochial unionism obsolete, these unions arose not so much because of the Civil War as in spite of it.

The great war was a disaster to most workers. Certainly it brought no economic salvation to American labor. A *New York Times* survey in 1869 reported that only one-eighth of the working classes earned sufficient income to afford the "comforts of life." A group of similar size could manage all the necessities. But three-quarters of the workers were found to earn "a meager subsistence . . . their families crowded [together in] slum apartments and boarding houses," their standard of living far short of a decent minimum.

During the three-quarters of a century between 1790 and 1865, American workers had helped make the United States one of the two leading industrial nations in the world. For all their signal contribution to America's welfare, however, most workers enjoyed neither influence nor well-being. At the war's end American society was about to experience the dislocations that would accompany the nation's leap into a mature industrialism. Their experience in concerted action helped fortify American workers in meeting the shocks that awaited them.

J. W. Alexander, "Burning of the Round-House at Pittsburgh."
Library of Congress.

★ 3 ★

LABOR IN THE INDUSTRIAL ERA

by David Montgomery

When the Skeffingtons left famine-ridden Ireland, they were determined to change their lives for the better. They did not rest until they reached the gold fields of California. Wealth eluded them, however, and they with their son, Harry, who was born in 1858, headed eastward to Philadelphia. When Harry was 13, they sent him to Portage, Wisconsin, to study for the priesthood. But he was destined to preach a different gospel from that which his parents had intended.

Within a year the lad had returned to Philadelphia to try his hand as an apprentice at a number of trades. He soon settled on shoemaking, because that "gentle craft" had become so thoroughly subdivided that even the most skilled operations, such as cutting the leather and guiding the lasted shoes through a McKay stitching machine, could be mastered in a few months.

At work he learned of a secret order, the name of which could not be told to Skeffington until he joined. Dedicated to the "Universal Brotherhood of Labor," it was the Noble and Holy Order of the Knights of Labor. Its leader was a garment cutter and one-time Baptist minister named Uriah Stephens. He preached that poverty and the competition for survival, which young Skeffington saw all about him in the city, represented "an artificial and man-created condition, not God's arrangement and order." It could be remedied only if working people learned "to respect industry in the person of every intelligent worker; beget concert of action by conciliation; confidence by just and upright conduct toward each other; mutual respect by dignified deportment; and wise counsels by what of wisdom and ability God, in his wisdom and goodness, has endowed us with."

Philadelphia's shoe industry was then dominated by thirty modern factories, despite the persistence of hundreds of custom shoemakers and more than 400 "sky parlors," where little groups stitched shoes in lofts. Competition from factories reduced the sky parlors to sweatshop conditions and drove custom shoemakers to the brink of despair. In the factories themselves, workers complained that they were forced to bribe foremen for jobs, faced periodic layoffs, and had to submit to frequent reductions in piece rates.

When Harry applied for membership in Local Assembly 64 of the Knights of Labor, he was turned down as too young. So for two years he listened to the older Knights where he worked, who could discuss their beliefs if not the business of their secret order. He was spellbound by the public spokesman of the shoe workers' assembly, English immigrant Thomas Phillips, who was old enough to be Skeffington's father. A veteran of the Chartist movement in his home country and of antislavery activities in Philadelphia, Phillips had founded a group of cooperative stores during the Civil War years; he subsequently emerged as a guiding spirit in an earlier shoemakers' union and in the International Workingmen's Association. He and Skeffington were soon to form a partnership in organizing shoe workers, which would last until the great depression of the 1890s.

On his eighteenth birthday, Harry underwent the mysterious ritual which made him a Knight, and before the year was out he had been elected Master Workingman of Local Assembly 64. The local had more than 750 members in 1881, when it commissioned Harry to organize the city's largest shoe firm, John Mundell and Co. Obtaining a job in its sole-cutting room, Skeffington soon discovered the most vexing grievance of its workers. After every seasonal layoff, the company welcomed back its old hands with the news that work was available, but at such low prices that workers would have to accept a temporary wage reduction. Invariably they agreed to produce at lower piece rates. After several months the former rates were restored, as promised. But, as the workers soon learned, that meant the next seasonal layoff was at hand.

Harry stealthily enrolled the cutters into the Knights and convinced them to reject any wage reduction at the beginning of the next season. Taken by surprise, the company restored full pay to the cutters but tried to compensate for its loss by lowering rates of women who marked or stitched parts. That decision prompted Mary Stirling to jump onto her bench and summon the women with whom she worked to walk out. Waving their aprons defiantly, they marched off, vowing to return only at full wages. Skeffington then called upon the men not to be outdone by the women. Down the stairs tramped the cutters, singing and calling the other men out.

For several weeks none of Mundell's 700 employees came to work. The women formed a local assembly of their own (despite the fact that officially the Knights did not admit women) and named it the Garfield Assembly, in honor of the recently assassinated President. They combined picket duty with fundraising bazaars and concerts at the assembly's hall. Soon they had neighborhood employers raging at Mundell to settle, because their own workers were going to the strike festivities instead of their jobs. In September Mary Stirling and other women accompanied Skeffington to the Knights' General Assembly in Cincinnati and persuaded the delegates to open the Order's doors officially to women.

When victory came at Mundell, it established the power of the Knights of Labor firmly in Philadelphia's shoe industry. By 1884 eleven local assemblies, ranging in size from 55 members to 1,000 and each representing different crafts or cluster of occupations, formulated wage demands and work rules for their respective members. Each assembly sent three delegates to District Assembly 70, the highest governing body for Philadelphia shoe workers. Within each factory a "shop union" elected by the workers in that plant handled grievances and enforced the rules of the local assemblies. To keep track of the myriad piece rates spawned by all the styles in this business, each plant had one male and one female statistician.

Grievances which could not be resolved by the shop union were sent to a city-wide arbitration committee, on which sat seven Knights and seven employers.

The workers increased their demands steadily. They shortened the time given employers to reply through the arbitration system, and they refused to work in the same factory with any employee who did not belong to the Order. Sudden strikes, which the workers called "vacations," were chronic, as workers settled old scores and drove the employers to fury. Finally, in October, 1887, the Shoe Manufacturers' Association, responding to a stoppage by 160 hand-sewing benchmen, fired all employees and refused to take any back until they repudiated the Knights of Labor. For a month and a half the hungry workers held out, then craft by craft they began to break ranks. By December the plants had reopened on the companies' terms.

The rise and fall of the power of organized workers in Philadelphia's shoe industry was duplicated in one industry after another during the last decades of the nineteenth century. Unionism achieved its greatest strength among coopers and anthracite coal miners in the early 1870s, among longshoremen, packing-house workers, iron and steel workers, and bituminous miners in the mid-1880s, and among iron molders, railroad workers, and building tradesmen in the early 1890s. But the style of operation displayed by the shoe workers and their ultimate defeat when business organized for battle typified the age.

Labor activists of Skeffington's time were the off-spring of the new America being created by modern industry. Few of them grew up on farms, and most were born in this country. A disproportionately large minority was made up of immigrants from England, it is true, for it was the home of the world's most highly developed union movement. The unions of coal miners, iron and steel workers, and northern textile workers adhered closely to many British practices. But most of the labor leaders of the time were raised in American towns or cities, were children of immigrant workers, and started working around the age of fourteen, after five or six years of schooling.

By the 1880s as many as half of them were Roman Catholics, though people active in the labor movement were reluctant to talk about religion.

These sons and daughters of early industrial America grew up in a world which, as Uriah Stephens had said, was "an artificial and man-created condition." The landmarks of their youth were not hills, springs, and oak groves, but taverns, meeting halls, market buildings, and roundhouses. Most workers lived close by countless chimneys which belched black smoke into the air. Their children swam in polluted rivers and ponds. Ironically, pollution in smaller factory towns was often worse than the notorious filth of New York and Chicago, because raw sewage was dumped directly into the local river, and barge canals made convenient trash dumps. Victorian town regulations often added to the bleakness of the surroundings. Robert Layton of Pittsburgh told Congress in 1883 that on Sundays, the workers' only day off, municipal ordinances in his town closed the libraries, while "our shop-keepers, who have pretty pictures or paintings in their windows, usually hang something over them in observance of the Sabbath."

When most of Skeffington's colleagues had been born, the population of the United States had just surpassed that of Great Britain, by reaching a total of some twenty million. Before most of them died, the country would have more than ninety million people. Between 1870 and 1910 the population rose by 132 percent, but the number of people involved in industrial labor soared even more rapidly—from 3,500,000 to 14,200,000. More than a fifth of the workers in 1870 were involved in construction alone, but their numbers over the next forty years did not increase as dramatically as those in other occupations. Iron and steel workers increased by over 1,200 percent between 1870 and 1910 to 326,000. Fabricators of goods from metals constituted almost twelve percent of the industrial labor force by 1910, after a forty-year growth of 437 percent. And more than half a million men were needed by the end of the century just to drive the horses and wagons delivering goods around congested city streets.

The growing economy drew millions of newcomers to jobs in American industry. Tens of thousands of French Canadians took trains to the textile, shoe, or paper towns of New England, where they lived in cramped tenements. For those migrants, one company official noted, the "country mill is generally a graduating school for the city mill." By the mid-1880s Manchester, Lowell, and Lawrence were each inhabited by several thousand *Québecois*. Similarly, black laborers from Virginia and the Carolinas moved through the Appalachians as railroad track crews, artisans, and coal miners. Like the French Canadians, they tended to return home for harvests and holidays, but many contractors preferred them because, as one said, the blacks "had a wider experience than these roadside white people, who do not stir out of their woods." White farm youths who moved to the cities shunned factory jobs to drive wagon teams and streetcars. The sons of more prosperous farmers often took advantage of their rural schooling to become printers, telegraphers, and clerks.

Twelve million other people boarded ships to come to America between 1865 and 1900. About half were Germans and Irish, and almost a million were British, many of whom had gained industrial experience in Europe. Each period of economic boom drew thousands of unskilled workers to American industry. By the 1880s American steamship and railroad agents had combed southeastern Europe, luring passengers for their ships and trains with promises of abundant work in the New World. Young men from the villages of Croatia, Galicia, the Carpathians, and the Italian *Mezzogiorno* left home in search of industrial wages. Settled communities of Ukranians, Italians, Poles, and Magyars soon became familiar sights in the United States, as many migrants sent home for their families. After 1890 these new arrivals came to outnumber those from Germany and Ireland.

Although the many nationalities mingled daily at work, in matters close to home they tended to cling to their own traditions. Intermarriage rates were extremely low. The center of each neighborhood was its church, where on the Lord's Day was heard the familiar liturgy from a clergyman who knew the language and ways not only of the home country but of the home village. Fraternal associations arose quickly to provide mutual insurance against the unpredictable ravages of an industrial economy and a defense against the cultural condescension of native Americans. All of them sought at least to "take charge of the body" when a countryman died.

Understandably, immigrants organized their lives more along ethnic lines than those of occupation. At one level, every neighborhood had its rival gangs—Bulldogs, Modocs, Chain Gang, Invincibles, Reedies, Schuylkill Rangers—which ruled the local turf to the terror of all strangers. At another, a crisis would bring the entire national community together, as happened when some newly arrived Germans were hooted by strikers for crossing picket lines at the Lackawanna Coal and Iron Company in 1872. In a mass meeting of Germans in the region, all vowed to defend each other and to march to work in a body. Joining strikes was as much a community action as breaking them. When thousands of Poles, Lithuanians, and Ruthenians walked out in support of the unions during the anthracite strike of 1888-89, the platform at an immigrant rally in the Shenandoah opera house was shared by a Greek Catholic priest, Lithuanian and Slovak merchants, the editors of the region's Lithuanian and Ruthenian papers, and a Polish shoemaker.

The concentration of industrial power was increasingly difficult for native and immigrant workers to resist. By the eve of the Civil War the United States had a manufacturing output second only to that of Great Britain. An elaborate railroad system, iron-hulled steamships, and electric telegraphs linked the northern and central parts of the country into a single market. Factory production prevailed in textiles, paper, and farm equipment. Prodigious accumulations of capital were at the disposal of eastern merchants and bankers for industrial investment. During the four decades following the war, the fabrication of the metal machinery, rails, and utensils on which a modern economy rests became a mechanized factory process. The United States census, which counted only 55,000 machinists in 1870, listed 283,000 of them in 1900. Through their efforts reapers, sewing machines, locomotives, air brakes, electrical streetcars, incandescent lamps, and bicycles became common. Machine-made machinery allowed the country's industrial output to outstrip that of England by 1885.

Capital needed to purchase the new equipment and set it in motion was raised by the incorporation of manufacturing concerns and the arrangement of elaborate partnerships. Moreover, the new larger firms safeguarded themselves against the unpredictability of competitive markets by various combinations. Those supplying consumer goods to urban markets—meat packers, for example—usually linked themselves together in price-fixing arrangements called trusts. Manufacturers of producers' goods often formed "vertical" combinations, such as the partnership of Henry Clay Frick's coke and William B. Oliver's iron with Andrew Carnegie's steelworks. In these types of arrangements workers faced increasingly powerful employers.

Nevertheless, much of American manufacturing continued to be carried on in small, even tiny, units. The construction and clothing industries were mosaics of small competitive enterprise, interlocked by elaborate webs of subcontracting. Although prefabrication of molding, doors, and other building parts was concentrated in large planing and rolling mills, the bricklaying, carpentry, plumbing, and plastering firms customarily remained small, providing avenues of upward mobility for immigrants and their children.

Men's clothing was mostly sewn by tailors in their homes, after the cloth had been cut to patterns in the manufacturer's shop. The invention of the sewing machine made the home a little factory. It even diminished the degree of control tailors had formerly exercised over their own hours of work, because, as tailor Conrad Carl pointed out, the "machine makes too much noise in the place, and the neighbors want to sleep, and we have to stop sewing earlier; so we have to work faster."

Carl sewed alongside his wife and daughter in their apartment. But many of the 18,000 tailors in New York were themselves employed by fellow tailors who, as Carl said, "get more work for themselves, and take it home and employ poor men and women." This was the infamous sweatshop system. By modifying the traditional pattern of working with his family only slightly, a tailor became a petty boss, obtaining his income from the difference between what he was paid for the sewing by the manufacturer and what he in turn paid his "helpers."

During the period between the Civil War and the

end of the century most American workers enjoyed a significant rise in the standard of living. Wartime inflation was followed by the depression of 1873-78 and the economic boom of the early 1880s. However, the general trend between 1878 and 1898 was one of steady wage levels and slowly falling food prices. Because food consumed more than half of the family budget of most workers, a reduction in the price of meat, flour, and potatoes freed a growing share of workers' incomes for clothes, housing, and a few of the pleasures of life.

Despite the long-term trend of improvement, all workers and their families suffered tangibly from the chronic threat of unemployment, the contempt of their social "betters," and the squalor of urban life. Unemployment was endemic to the new industrial order. True, working people had always experienced alternating seasons of intense work and relative idleness. The regular winter layoffs of coal miners in the 1880s were caused by frozen waterways, and the huge Amoskeag textile mill in New Hampshire was shut down for three weeks when a local drought reduced the level of the Merrimac River, curtailing power. But such natural causes of unemployment were becoming far less important than those growing out of the workings of a modern economy. Shifting seasonal demands, crippling illnesses caused by industrial poisons, and alternating spasms of relentless work and forced idleness caused by the drive of each employer to capture as much of the market as possible—all these made for many long days without income.

In fact, the entire economy progressed in spurts. For

example, record-breaking sales of American wheat to
Europe in 1878 stimulated a boom. Coal and iron
output soared as new railroad lines were laid at
breakneck pace. Germans came to American factories
in numbers matching those of the early 1850s. Nor-
wegians, Swedes, and Danes immigrated at rates
reaching 100,000 a year, and many of them headed
straight for the wheat lands. As American grain began
to undersell Hungarian wheat even at the port of
Trieste, peasant youth from southeastern Europe
boarded ships to seek work in the United States.

Early in 1883 the bubble burst. Dozens of railroads
went bankrupt, and more than twenty-two banks
failed. Immigration fell off by more than one-third,
and thousands of newcomers returned home.

There were two major depressions—one lasting
from 1873 to 1878 and the other from 1893 to 1897.
In both crises, national levels of unemployment surpassed sixteen percent of the labor force. Although
bread, soup, and old clothing were made available
by private charities, many unemployed workers shared
the defiant pride of the hungry miner who said: "We
are American citizens and we don't go to hospitals
and poorhouses." Most wandered from town to town
in search of work. Municipal authorities complained
of the multitudes of "tramps," who would appear in
their communities and, by an elaborate code of marks
placed on walls or fences, leave notices about the
location of generous householders or fierce dogs.

For many more workers depressions meant wage
cuts and short time. Between 1893 and 1898, for
example, Pennsylvania's anthracite miners averaged

no more than 178 workdays each year. Gardens and hunting helped them survive. A mule spinner from Fall River told a Senate committee in the fall of 1883 that he had worked only 113 days since the previous Thanksgiving. One of his sons had "one shoe on, a very poor one, and a slipper, that was picked up somewhere. The other has two odd shoes, with the heel out. He has got cold and is sickly now." His wife had a dress, the one in which she had been married, and saved it for church. Someone had given her a chemise and "an old wrapper, which is about a mile too big for her." The house was heated by driftwood, collected from the seashore, and the family dined largely on chowder, made from clams found in the same place, and bread. A friend once had the family over for a Sunday dinner of roast pork.

It was easy for the more fortunate members of society to blame such sufferings on the "ignorance, indolence, and immorality" of the poor. They believed that this was a land of "self-made men," in which earnest effort could carry any ambitious youth up the ladder of success. The upper and middle classes concluded that anyone who seriously wanted work could find it in America; those who failed were simply too demanding. In the literature of the age, workers were often portrayed as dullards or as dangerous, drunken louts. John Hay's "good workman" in *The Bread-winners* was "sober, industrious, and unambitious," and "contented with his daily work and wages." The story's labor agitator had eyes "too sly and furtive to belong to an honest man." Inhabitants of a city's tenements, described by Helen Campbell and two

fellow civic reformers in *Darkness and Daylight: Or,
Lights and Shadows of New York Life,* were depicted
as ". . . a class apart, the poor Irish forming by far
the larger proportion. They retain all the most brutal
characteristics of the Irish peasant at home, but without the redeeming lightheartedness. . . . Sullen,
malicious, conscienceless, with no capacity for enjoy-
ment save in drink and the lowest forms of debauch-
ery, they are filling our prisons and reformatories,
marching in an ever-increasing number through the
quiet country, and making a reign of terror wherever
their footsteps are heard. With a little added intelli-
gence they become Socialists, doing their heartiest
to ruin the institutions by which they live."

The workers' sense of social class was forged as
much by their awareness of the contempt in which
they were held by "their betters" as by economic
deprivation. When the worker is "at work," labor reformer George E. McNeill wrote, "he belongs to the
lower orders, and is continually under surveillance;
when out of work, he is an outlaw, a tramp,—he is a
man without the rights of manhood,—the pariah of
society, homeless, in the deep significance of the term."

Many small property holders in industrial towns
were as resentful of the pretentions of the business
elite as were the workers. In strikes local shopkeepers
and professional men often sided with the strikers
against "alien corporations," like railroads, and the
town's own leading industrialists. They shared with
the workers elements of a popular culture, in which
one never spoke of "lower classes," but of the "working," "industrious," or "producing" classes.

The praise they bestowed on the "honest mechanics" of their communities echoed through the popular songs and dime-novel literature of the day. For ten cents, workers could find themselves heroically portrayed in stories like *Larry Locke: Man of Iron, Or, A Fight for Fortune, A Story of Labor and Capital,* and *Jasper Ray: The Journeyman Carpenter, Or, One Man as Good as Another in America.* They could sing around the piano to the strains of "Daddy Was Killed by the Pinkerton Men," while the rugged face of Rolling Mill John Kelly, whose music hall performances had made the song famous, beamed at them from the title page. Although this culture was infused with a populist, rather than a strictly class consciousness, it clearly separated the nation into "the producers" and "the exploiters."

The burden of social condescension, deprivation, and toil fell most severely on the working-class woman. Although more than one-fourth of the non-agricultural wage earners of the country were women from 1870 onward, a study conducted by the Commissioner of Labor in 1885 found that eighty percent of the wage-earning women were single and lived in family homes. Even in such industries as textiles, shoes, and clothing, where forty to sixty percent of the workers might be women, most of them were young and childless, or widows. The leading occupation for women (in fact, the largest occupational group in the economy) was domestic service, at which almost 914,000 women worked in 1870. It was practically an expected part in the life cycle of teen-age

Irish and German immigrants that they would serve in some prosperous household until they married.

A few women found their way into relatively skilled occupations. Significant numbers of women were in telegraph operating and printing, where they were often relatives of men working in the trades. The International Typographical Union not only admitted women to membership, but even boasted a woman Corresponding Secretary in 1870. The craft which produced the most effective unionism of women, however, was that of the collar starchers of Troy, New York. First organized in 1864 and subsequently represented in the National Labor Union by Kate Mullaney, the women of Troy briefly operated their own cooperative laundry and continued their unionism recurrently until they were crushed in the strike of 1905. In 1886 more than 8,000 laundry and shirt workers struck under the leadership of the collar starchers' Joan of Arc Assembly of the Knights of Labor.

The working woman with a family faced the double burden of household and factory chores. "Let's swallow our dinner, and, when we have time, chew it," one such woman advised her companions in the factory. Male labor reformers advocated keeping married women home and paying their husbands enough to maintain the family in decency. "There is a greater necessity than all others that our industrial system shall be so regulated that the head of a family shall be permitted to preserve his family intact," argued Frank K. Foster, "and that the labor of women and girls and children to the large extent which I have described shall not be so important a factor in the production of our manufacturing industries."

But even if workers accomplished that goal, the housewife hardly found the home a place of relaxation. The coal stove, which provided heat and cooking, needed endless stoking. Marketing had to be done daily. Mending clothes, baking bread, and other tasks consumed countless hours. If the home had any room to spare, it was likely occupied by boarders, for whom the housewife cooked and washed.

To make matters worse, most industrial towns financed their municipal improvements by levies on the residents of the areas which benefited directly from them. This meant that sewer systems, decent water supplies, lighting, and even paving were seldom available in workers' neighborhoods. Consequently, housekeeping involved a ceaseless struggle against filth, fought with rags, ammonia, and buckets of water carried up staircases from outside hydrants.

A wide variety of living standards could be found among industrial workers in the latter part of the nineteenth century. It was evident that the gradual increase in real incomes was enjoyed more by some workers than by others. By the end of the 1880s an income of roughly $500 a year would have been necessary for a family of five in a middle-sized industrial town to enjoy any of life's amenities (newspapers, beer, lodge membership, outings, tobacco) without literally depriving themselves of basic necessities. About forty percent of the working-class families earned less than that. Those families, crowded into one or two rooms in poor tenements, depended heavily on the earnings of their children. About one-fourth of them lived in total destitution. Many found their living by scavenging, begging, and hustling.

The largest group of workers (some forty-five percent) had incomes which, in good times, clung precariously above the poverty level. Molders, carpenters, machinists, mule spinners, and coal miners might manage a house or flat of four to five rooms (more, if they took in boarders) and put plenty of cheaper meat, potatoes, bread, and vegetables on the table, if the mother managed the budget skillfully and the father avoided illness or injury. Recreation, largely that provided by the workers for themselves, included cards, dominoes, baseball, horseshoes, and a convivial pitcher of beer. Textile towns abounded in reading rooms, gymnasiums, and debating clubs, where drinking, gambling, and profanity were strictly forbidden. In summer, unions often threw grand parades and picnics for the entire community. Temperance societies and lodges of the Grand Army of the Republic, the *Liederkranz,* or the Caledonia Club provided for other outings. Many a worker might be indifferent to unions, observed William Strauss of the Tailors' Union, but "mention to him an organization of the social club order, where political debates, occasional hops, entertainments, and receptions are the principal features, and he is all attention at once."

Among the most prosperous workers, including many iron rollers, locomotive engineers, pattern makers, and glass blowers, incomes ran from $800 to $1,100 yearly. Many union men within this top fifteen percent of the working class toiled at tasks both physically exhausting and demanding high levels of experience and judgment. James Parton, a columnist, saw iron craftsmen in Pittsburgh working so hard that they had "to stop, now and then, in summer, take off their boots and *pour the perspiration out of them.*"

These men, said Parton, were the true "aristocracy of labor." Their wives tended tidy homes not far from the mills. When the availability of rapid transit systems enabled the middle classes to leave the smoky cities for quieter suburbs, working-class craftsmen replaced them as the recognized leaders of the urban communities.

Factory discipline and the neighborhoods in which they lived provided workers with a common core of experience. They had jobs while middle and upper classes had careers. The younger worker, after leaving school at age fourteen or younger, usually reached his highest earnings by the time he was in his mid-twenties. From that point on, barring calamity, his standard of living was molded by two things: the ages of his children and the fortunes of his trade. As the number of mouths increased, the family would be forced to scrimp and save until the day when the children were old enough to work. "When people own houses," observed John Keogh, a printer of Fall River, "you will generally find that it is a large family all working together." In old age, when few men could hold on to better-paying jobs, the worker was at the mercy of his children or the county poorhouse.

Children of business and professional families tended to stay in school longer. They began working

at low incomes and moved by stages toward the expected prosperity of their class. Such expectations
promoted a drive for achievement, at least for boys,
and made it easy for them to accept the society's
dominant code of acquisitive individualism. On the
other hand, the optimistic mentality, fostered by
middle-class life experience, made it difficult if not
impossible to comprehend the demands of workers
for regulation of working conditions by trade union
and governmental action, both of which seemed to
"stifle individual initiative." As E. L. Godkin edi-
torialized in *The Nation:* "Labor never was, and never
can be, injured by capital, so long as both are left free
from governmental and other arbitrary interference
or action." Unlimited opportunity to rise was the highest ideal of this segment of society, and the "self-
made man" was its cultural hero.

Spokesmen of the late nineteenth-century labor
movement denounced the ideology of acquisitive individualism with ardor. "Whoever gets rich does so from
other means than simply 'energy and perseverance'
to earn," charged the editors of Boston's labor paper
the *Daily Evening Voice* in 1867. "Something that he
does not earn—something that another earns—must
be added to give wealth, and therefore, in proportion
as one grows rich, those who produce the riches he
gets must become poor." It is wrong to inspire people
with the desire to "be capitalists," the editorial concluded, because that aspiration sets everyone at war
with his neighbor. "It is the high and holy mission
of labor reform to show to men an object worthier
than wealth," the creation of a more equitable society.

> *The time has come to stand erect,*
> *In noble, manly self-respect;*
> *To see the bright sun overhead,*
> *To feel the ground beneath our tread;*
> *Unled by priests, uncursed by creeds,*
> *Our manhood proving by our deeds.*

So began a poem often recited by Knights of Labor orator Richard F. Trevellick. Its defiant egalitarianism reappeared incessantly in music-hall songs, speeches to workingmen's clubs, and odes recited by children at lodge picnics. The poem concluded by blending its evangelical theme of self-improvement into that of struggle for social reform:

> *Let Agitation come; who fears?*
> *We need the flood; the filth of years*
> *Has gathered round us. Roll then on.*
> *What cannot stand had best be gone.*

When the leaders of labor organizations in the late nineteenth century described their goals, they seldom limited their discussion to higher wages and shorter hours. Far more frequently they spoke of "the emancipation of the working class" or "the abolition of the wages system" as their ultimate purpose. To socialists such phrases implied the extinction of private ownership of industrial enterprise. More conservative figures, like President John Oberly of the Typographical Union—who believed that "capital is the golden egg that enriches labor"—advocated the thorough organization of workers, so that they might be able to command their own conditions and overcome "that cruel law of supply and demand." But radical and moderate labor advocates alike agreed that the most

ominous menace to all they held dear was the growing concentration of business enterprise. An appeal of
the American Federation of Labor in 1888 warned of
"the fast-coming grand struggle between Capital and
Labor, involving the perpetuation of the civilization
we have so laboriously evolved." George E. McNeill
stressed the political implications of that belief in *The
Labor Movement: The Problem of To-Day:* "We declare that there is an inevitable and irresistible conflict
between the wage-system of labor and the republican
system of government—the wage-laborer attempting
to save the government, and the capitalist class ignor-
antly attempting to subvert it."

During these decades, workers created a wide variety of institutions, all of them infused with a spirit
of mutuality. Through their fraternal orders, cooperatives, reform clubs, political parties, and trade unions,
American workers shaped a collectivist counter-culture
in the midst of the growing factory system.

Fraternal orders and cooperative societies enjoyed
great popularity, though neither restricted their membership to wage workers. In fact, fraternal lodges
tended to group people along ethnic or religious lines.
They brought some shopkeepers and professional men
together with manual workers, as did the Ancient
Order of Hibernians, St. Lawrence Society, *Turn-
vereins,* and Caledonian Society. Other orders, like the
Knights of Pythias and the Father Matthew Total
Abstinence Union, were tied to the temperance movement. Later in the century, several unions experimented with death and unemployment benefits, imi-
tating the practice of major British unions; but they

never became successful competitors of fraternal orders in this field. A greater threat to the benefit schemes of fraternal orders and unions alike was commercial life insurance, which became available in the 1880s for small weekly premiums.

Cooperatives faced similar challenge from installment credit and mail-order selling in commercial enterprise. Numerous cooperative stores appeared in the 1870s, especially in textile and mining areas heavily populated by British immigrants. They were encouraged by the spread of Granges among farmers, the formation of the Sovereigns of Industry, which had ninety-six councils promoting such stores, and later by the Co-operative Board of the Knights of Labor. Some of these enterprises were informal "dividing stores," where groups of families bought staples at wholesale prices. The giant Fall River store, which occupied an entire block, was described by the prominent British cooperator George J. Holyoake as larger than anything in England.

Factories cooperatively owned by their operatives sprang up like mushrooms between 1868 and 1873, and again between 1880 and 1885. Most of them were iron foundries, shoe companies, and cooperage works, though ship carpenters and caulkers founded two large dry dock companies. After 1880 the Co-operative Board of the Knights of Labor provided advice, advertising, and some financial assistance to such enterprises. Among those it aided were a tobacco factory in Raleigh, a barrel works in St. Louis, a piano company, a canning association, several cigar companies, a sardine packer, a paint works, a soap works, a broom manufacturer, and the Persian Cement and Handy Mucilage Company. Few of these concerns were successful raising working capital from their members. The enterprises that did turn a profit often saw their founders succumb to the lure of individualism, destroying the cooperative's original objectives. Yet the faith remained strong:

> One sure way to make a cure
> And solve this labor question;
> With heads and hands to tie the bands
> In steps of Co-operation.

Although both reformist and revolutionary workers' political parties played important roles in the development of the labor movement and its ideology, neither seriously threatened the hegemony of the Republican and Democratic parties in the electoral system. Labor reform parties arose locally in Pittsburgh, Cincinnati, and LaSalle, Illinois, in the late 1860s, and in dozens of communities between 1886 and 1888. The trade unionists who led them twice fused their efforts with those of farmers' organizations to produce effective national parties—the Greenback Labor (or National) Party of the late seventies and the People's Party of the early nineties. The enthusiastic crowds these parties often drew tended to return to their traditional party allegiances on Election Day.

During the 1880s the Democrats had risen steadily to the status of the majority party of the North on the basis of their defense of cultural diversity in local controversies over schooling, liquor licensing, and blue laws. The root of their failure lay in the variety of the ethnic groups which waves of immigration had brought to America. The depression of the 1890s reversed that trend, because the Democrats were blamed for the hard times.

Numerous trade unionists and Knights of Labor gained state and local political offices through nominations by the major parties. In the early 1870s and throughout the 1880s, Republicans and Democrats alike eagerly snatched up prominent workers to be candidates in their own neighborhoods. Here was an important avenue of social advancement for ambitious workers, which played a major role in inhibiting the development of a national labor party.

Revolutionary organizations exerted a much greater influence on agitational campaigns than on electoral activity. The Socialist Labor Party, formed in 1876 from the remnants of some fifty sections of the earlier International Workingmen's Association, envisaged trade unions which "keep pace with the progress of the age and with the march of advanced ideas" as containing "the seed for a new and better system." So heavily was its influence concentrated in the central labor unions of major cities that all ten of the party members who attended the 1890 AFL convention were delegates from those bodies. Two major anarcho-communist groups had followings greater than that of the SLP in the mid-eighties— the Social Revolutionaries, led by Johann Most, and the Home Club of the Knights of Labor, whose fifty members were all leading officers of local assemblies in New York City. The Home Club's unique blending of revolutionary general unionism, cooperatives, and Irish nationalism gave it an important following during the upsurge of labor activity in 1885 and 1886.

The most durable of workers' organizations were the trade unions. They flourished when there was sufficient prosperity to provide them a fighting chance of success. Local unions numbering more than 1,000 members were rare, and many boasted no more than twenty to thirty people. There were few written contracts before the 1880s and fewer salaried officers. The members met frequently, decided on work rules and wage scales among themselves at the beginning of each session, and pledged not to work for less than they had resolved.

Although more than 300,000 workers participated in local unions of this type in 1872, their organizations often faced defeat and were short-lived. To increase their strength, unions combined both into national organizations of the same trade, like the Iron Molders' International Union, and into city-wide assemblies of delegates from many trades, like the Central Labor Union of New York. Eighteen national unions sent delegates, along with those of many local unions and other types of workers' societies, to annual sessions of the National Labor Union (later called the Industrial Congress) between 1866 and 1875, where a general program for the labor movement was formulated.

During those same years unions grew strong in the shoe, coal, construction, and mid-western iron industries. They staged spectacular strikes for the eight-hour day, climaxed by a partially successful walkout of 100,000 workers in New York during May and June, 1872.

The depression of 1873 wiped out these achievements, making so many people eager to work at any terms that few unions could enforce their rules. Secret societies often took the place of unions. In many coal patches, where the defeated miners' unions had once held sway, local assemblies of the Knights of Labor shielded their members from prying eyes by elaborate rituals and oaths of silence. A network of railroad brakemen's lodges remained unknown to the outside world until the great strikes of 1877. Sensational murder trials the previous year had brought the name "Molly Maguires" to the public eye and sent ten Irishmen to the gallows.

In late July, 1877, train crews on the Baltimore and Ohio Railroad struck against a wage cut, triggering a chain reaction of events which President Hayes was to condemn as an "insurrection." Popular anger over the dispatch of troops to reopen the line spread the strike to Baltimore, where huge crowds clashed with the militia. Simultaneously, work stoppages followed the rail lines across Pennsylvania from both ends of the state into the smallest mill and mining towns. Thousands of Pittsburgh iron workers and other residents defeated soldiers sent from Philadelphia in pitched battle, subsequently burning all property of the Pennsylvania Railroad. Across Ohio and Indiana, workers' committees simply took over their towns, halting all work until their demands were met by employers. A quickly organized strike in Chicago brought troops and artillery to the city, and shots rang out at the Halstead Street viaduct. In St. Louis, thousands of workers closed down the city's industry for several days. Governmental authorities fled the town. In San Francisco, great crowds sacked railroad property and attacked Chinatown.

Amid the funerals and prosecutions which followed in the wake of the great strikes of 1877, the Knights of Labor emerged as the most powerful organized body of workers in the land. A rapid influx of coal miners into what had been previously a secret society of Philadelphia craftsmen forced the Order to hold its first General Assembly in 1878, make its name public, and elect Terence V. Powderly of Scranton as General Master Workman. From then through 1883 it grew slowly, most of its members entering local assemblies of their own trades. But an important minority joined mixed assemblies, where all "producers" were welcomed. The Knights opposed strikes on principle and sanctioned them only in cases where members were victimized or employers refused to arbitrate. Those two categories, however, allowed hundreds of strikes to be waged under the Order's auspices. Craftsmen used their trades assemblies in much the same way as others used trade unions, and often sought to band their assemblies together into national trade districts, like those of the telegraphers and shoe workers. On the other hand, many prominent Knights, preferring to promote cooperatives and stress the educational role of the Order, were hostile toward strikes and union-type activity within their midst. In all, more than 15,000 local assemblies were organized between 1869 and 1895, at least one in almost every urban community in the land and 400 in New York City. Their members included glass blowers, domestics, and cowboys. Perhaps no other voluntary institution in

America, except churches, touched the lives of as many people as did the Knights of Labor.

The organizing impulse of the eighties also brought a revival of national trade unions and the formation in 1881 of the Federation of Organized Trades and Labor Unions. The Federation had been a rather insignificant body, devoted primarily to lobbying for legislation of interest to labor. Then Frank Foster of the Typographical Union and Peter J. McGuire of the Carpenters and Joiners convinced it to bid for the leadership of the union's economic struggles by launching a nationwide campaign to secure the eight-hour day by May 1, 1886. The ineffectiveness of the various state laws making eight hours "a legal day's work"— enacted in the 1860s—and the successful strikes of the New York building workers for shorter hours in 1884 convinced most unionists that only direct action could reduce their hours. But few leaders of national unions were prepared to commit themselves to an all-out battle, and Powderly warned the members of the Knights to remain aloof from the movement, which he considered foolhardy. Nevertheless, Eight Hour Leagues sprang up in many cities, organizing local unions and Knights' assemblies alike for the crusade, and both Socialists and Social Revolutionaries threw themselves wholeheartedly into the agitation.

Huge parades were staged on May 1, in Chicago, Milwaukee, New York, San Francisco, Cincinnati, and other industrial centers. So many employers conceded some reduction of hours (usually a nine-hour day) that about 185,000 workers benefited. In addition to the many strikes for shorter hours, southern textile workers, Connellsville coke workers, southwestern railroad shop men, and others totaling more than 690,000 participated in strikes that year. Membership in both the unions and the Knights grew rapidly.

These strikes inspired great anxiety among the more prosperous members of society. Their attentions were focused on the trial of eight Social Revolutionaries accused of conspiring to hurl a bomb into the ranks of policemen who had sought to break up an open-air rally in Chicago's Haymarket Square. The trial concluded with four men, among them Albert Parsons and August Spies, being sent to the gallows in November, 1887, to the thunderous applause of most of the nation's commercial press.

The new-found strength and prestige of the national unions of coal miners, cigar makers, carpenters, molders, iron and steel workers, and printers, seconded by their need to defend themselves in jurisdictional conflicts with the rapidly expanding Knights, prompted them to create the American Federation of Labor in December, 1886. It replaced the moribund Federation of Organized Trades and Labor Unions. Although the new Federation recognized the autonomy of each national union in the control of its trade, it was better designed to wage economic struggles than the old Federation had been. Headed by Samuel Gompers and Peter McGuire, it set out to help the formation of new unions, lure national trade districts of the Knights into its fold, and mobilize its constituent unions for mutual assistance in a renewed campaign for the eight-hour day.

The six major unions of the AFL together had scarcely 200,000 members in 1888, and the Federation itself operated out of Gompers's tiny office. The key to its early strength lay not in its size or funds, but in the remarkable propensity of craftsmen to quit work when their union rules were violated and to engage in sympathy strikes to aid other workers.

Early in the 1890s, employers in one industry after another challenged this militant craft unionism frontally. None of the resulting conflicts captured public attention quite like the showdown in Andrew Carnegie's great steelworks at Homestead, near Pittsburgh. When the 700 craftsmen of the Amalgamated Iron and Steel Workers' lodge were locked out, more than 3,000 nonunion workers stood by them through six months of striking and a furious gun battle with Pinkerton detectives. Four other Carnegie plants and several mills unrelated to the steel company also stopped work in sympathy. In the end, however, new hands were brought into the Homestead mill under the protection of the state militia, and the union was forced to surrender.

Less public attention was bestowed on an even more significant battle in the South that same summer. Because the weakest links in the chain of labor solidarity were found at the points where the white, black, and yellow races met, the numerous episodes of cooperation between white and black workers during the 1880s provided a noteworthy feature of the labor upsurge. Although a number of trade unions had appeared among blacks immediately after the Civil War, and some of them had participated in the National Labor

Union, it was in the eighties that large numbers of blacks first unionized, especially among dock workers, coal miners, and construction workers in the South. The Knights alone had some 60,000 black members by 1886. More than a fifth of the early members of United Mine Workers in the bituminous fields were black. In 1896, Richard L. Davis, a black leader from Ohio, won the highest vote of any candidate for that union's National Executive Board.

The New Orleans docks were a stronghold of bi-racial unionism. When the white scalemen and packers there allied with the black teamsters to strike for a ten-hour day in October, 1892, the city's Board of Trade offered concessions to the whites but refused to negotiate with blacks. In response, forty-nine unions shut down the entire city and kept it shut, despite venomous attacks on the blacks in the local press. In the end, the Board of Trade capitulated entirely, giving labor one of its greatest victories of the century. Immediately afterward, the newly enacted Sherman Antitrust Act was put to its first use, and the New Orleans unions were convicted of violating it.

The sympathy strike was the most provocative manifestation of mutuality in practice. Although it enraged businessmen, sympathetic action gave workers such strength that it was hailed by Eugene V. Debs of the American Railway Union as "the hope of civilization and the supreme glory of mankind." A battle waged by Debs's own union provided the ultimate confrontation between that weapon and the entire organized force of the new industrial establishment.

The ARU had grown rapidly after the outbreak of

the great depression in 1893 as a new organization with an almost messianic appeal embracing all grades of railroad workers. When its convention met, in June, 1894, representatives of strikers at the Pullman Car Company asked for help. They received a pledge that the union would boycott all Pullman cars, allowing none to move on American railroads. The General Managers' Association of all railroads entering Chicago responded to the challenge by ordering that Pullman cars be attached to trains wherever possible and that any worker who refused to handle them be fired. By early July, a total strike had settled in over the railroads of the middle and far West, bringing in quick sequence a federal injunction against the strike, the stationing of troops at all vital junctions of the lines, martial law in Chicago, and the imprisonment of Debs and other strike leaders.

The great strike was crushed by the armed might of the government. Labor had to retreat or escalate the battle to a national strike of sympathy with the railwaymen. Several thousand workers had already walked out when the executives of thirty-four unions met in Chicago to consider their course of action. After intense debate, the leaders advised their members not to strike. Noting the "array of armed force and brutal monied aristocracy," represented by "United States Marshals, injunctions of courts, proclamations by the President, and . . . bayonets of soldiers," they concluded that it would be "worse than folly to call men out on a general or local strike in these days of stagnant trade and commercial depression" into confrontation with the government itself. The power of sympathy had been defused.

Hardly seven years later, union membership again rose rapidly in a setting of buoyant prosperity to levels unheard of in the nineteenth century. Chicago in 1900 saw more workers on strike than had been out during the Pullman Boycott. Two years later the coal miners won a major victory over the anthracite operators, with some help from government intervention. But the sympathy strike was then declared "outlaw" by the leaders of the AFL, who had come to rely upon "sacred contracts" and union labels for their security. In fact, Gompers and his colleagues were seeking to cooperate with eminent business leaders in search of a formula by which organized labor might become an accepted part of the new industrial order.

Titanic struggles lay ahead for labor, especially between 1916 and 1922 and between 1934 and 1941, but those efforts would require new styles of organization and activity. The workers' culture of the late nineteenth century, the militant craft unionism it produced, and its vision of a less acquisitive and competitive future society had all been relegated to history.

Industrial Workers of the World poster.
Library of Congress.

★ 4 ★

WORKERS OF
A NEW CENTURY

by Philip Taft

During the economic crisis that gripped the country in the early 1890s, farmers complained of low prices, businessmen of falling orders, and wage earners of salary cuts. Unemployment was widespread. Armies of jobless men swarmed over the countryside and rode freight trains. Bread lines and soup kitchens became commonplace.

The depression of the 1890s had softened the public attitude towards organized labor. Between 1897 and 1904, union membership climbed from 447,000 to 2,072,700. In the same period, the number of internationals affiliated with the American Federation of Labor (AFL) rose from fifty-eight to 120. The AFL had come on the scene in the 1880s, created by the leaders of craft unions who sought to curb invasions of their jurisdictions by the Knights of Labor. While the principal reason for embarking on this venture was defensive, AFL founders believed in the improvement of wages and working conditions through trade-union action—including the strike if necessary. Adolph Strasser, president of the International Cigar Makers Union, described the AFL program as a constant seeking of "more and more," a slogan frequently repeated by AFL President Samuel Gompers.

The early years of the century witnessed a stabilization of the labor movement, but it was also a time when some employers were determined to halt its further progress. One of the first challenges came from the steel industry. The Amalgamated Association of Iron and Steel Workers, established in the 1870s, saw its position endangered with the formation of the United States Steel Corporation in 1901. The convention of the union met that year and voted that each combine, or multiple companies, would be required to sign a union contract for all of its plants. This demand became the sticking point in negotiations. When no agreement was reached, the union called a strike in three of U.S. Steel's subsidiaries.

As the strike continued, a committee from the National Civic Federation, established for promoting the peaceful adjustment of labor disputes, intervened. The committee included Gompers, United Mine Workers President John Mitchell, and Senator Mark Hanna, President McKinley's mentor. A conference of strike leaders met with J.P. Morgan, Charles M. Schwab, and Elbert Gary, heads of the U.S. Steel Corporation. Morgan, denying hostility to unions, argued that it was not practicable for the corporation to recognize unions for unorganized mills. When the union leaders rejected his arguments, the companies began to replace the strikers.

At another meeting, Charles M. Schwab, speaking for the corporation, said that since many steel mills had been started by nonunion labor, the companies would only sign for mills which had not started up. The union was given twenty-four hours to accept; otherwise all negotiations would be terminated. On the plea of the Civic Federation Committee, Schwab extended the time, but the union would not immediately accept. The strike dragged on until September 14, 1901, when it was settled on terms disastrous to the union. Under the agreement, the union lost fourteen mills, but it suffered much more. It could not, in fact, seek to organize any mills.

The union's insistence upon signing all mills of a company was obviously ill-advised, since it could not be enforced. Amalgamated had overestimated its strength, and many steelworkers refused to follow its leadership. The effect of the 1901 strike was to strengthen the enemies of organized labor in the greatest center of economic power.

After the defeat of 1901, the union steadily lost strength. The puddlers, who became dissatisfied with the union's inclusion of all classes of steel labor, seceded and formed the Sons of Vulcan in 1907. The final blow fell when the American Sheet and Tin Plate Company posted a notice ". . . that all its plants after June 30, 1909, will be operated as 'open' plants." The Amalgamated had no choice but to call a strike. But it was a losing battle. The union surrendered after fourteen months.

"Inside," or company, unions were the employers' answer to organizing by bona fide unions. On the Great Lakes, where the U.S. Steel Corporation operated fleets of iron ore vessels, a company union, the Lake Carriers' Beneficial Association, was established in 1903 to "maintain, by contract or otherwise, such amicable relations between employer and employed as would avoid public injury that would result from lockouts or strikes. . . ." In the spring of 1908 the association declared for the open shop and voted to deny union delegates access to ships. An organized effort to deny employment to union members followed. The union fought back, and there were bloody clashes at lake ports. But it was difficult to overcome the combined resources of the shippers. When the association announced in 1912 that no discrimination would be directed against union members, the walkout ended. U.S. Steel extended its open-shop policies to other industries in which it had influence. One was bridge construction. The National Erectors' Association, organized in 1903, took U.S. Steel's lead and pledged to maintain the open shop. Subcontractors were expected to follow suit. Consequently, members of the International Association of Bridge and Structural Workers found themselves excluded from many jobs.

The union reacted by dynamiting nonunion jobs. From 1908 to 1911, they set off an estimated seventy explosions at unorganized jobs. In 1910, the *Los Angeles Times* building was dynamited, killing twenty. General Harrison Gray Otis, the publisher, blamed labor terrorists. The California State Federation of Labor charged the *Times* with laying the foundation for another Haymarket case, and denounced it "as a hostile and unscrupulous enemy, not only of unionism, but to progress generally."

The National Erectors' Association hired detective

William J. Burns to find out who was blowing up their bridges and buildings. He accused the union's secretary-treasurer, John H. McNamara, and his brother James. The prosecution charged that San Francisco unionists were trying to organize open-shop Los Angeles and that the *Times* stood in their way. Unionists, including Gompers, insisted the McNamara brothers were framed; Clarence Darrow was hired as defense counsel. But the McNamara brothers confessed, dealing labor a damaging blow.

Because of its vast resources the steel industry was able to impose its will on the unions of its employees and compel employers in other industries to follow its example. On the other hand, employers in the metal trades and foundries were not strong enough to resist organizational efforts of unions. In an attempt to promote harmonious relations with labor, the foundrymen producing cast-iron ware established the National Founders' Association in 1898. The National Metal Trades Association was set up in 1900 for similar purposes. In neither instance were the hopes for cooperation realized. In the case of the foundrymen and the International Molders' Union, differences were submitted to the presidents of the respective organizations and four members from each side. As a result, on issues of basic importance the parties deadlocked. In 1904 the Founders' Association decided to go its own way. The next few years witnessed many strikes in the foundries. Often there was violence because employers tried to keep their plants operating with replacements.

Employers established the National Metal Trades Association to find a basis of cooperation with the

International Association of Machinists, the dominant union in the industry. At the time, the union was seeking the nine-hour workday. The Murray Hill agreement between the association and the union, signed in New York City in May, 1900, stipulated that the hours of labor would be reduced to fifty-seven a week and to fifty-four within a year. Overtime rates were defined, apprenticeship regulated, and strikes and lockouts prohibited during the term of the agreement.

However, as soon as the contract was signed members of the union insisted that wages be raised to compensate for reduced hours of work. When negotiations reached an impasse, the National Metal Trades Association, on June 10, 1901, abrogated its contract with the International Association of Machinists, and the following week enunciated its Declaration of Principles.

The employer was to have complete and unrestricted control over the work force. The association declared, "It is the privilege of the employee to leave our employ whenever he sees fit and it is the privilege of the employer to discharge any workman he sees fit." The principles enunciated were embodied in the words "open shop," which meant that the employer was the absolute master. Under the code no interference with the prerogatives of management was tolerated.

Unions were combated by a combination of blacklisting, espionage, strikebreaking, and company unions. The National Metal Trades established labor bureaus in major cities for compiling records of employees in the industry so that the blacklist could be more effective. To promote the open shop, the National Metal Trades Association conducted the "investigation and adjustment of questions arising between members and their employees." This kind of activity consisted of using industrial spies in plants to disrupt labor unions and cause the dismissal of union activists. If a strike in the plant nevertheless followed, "the association assumed complete control over the settlement of the dispute in exchange for the strikebreaking services which it made available to the member." The association paid the cost of recruiting strikebreakers and the bonus needed to attract them.

Large single employers could successfully combat a labor organization and by various devices prevent its establishment on their properties. Smaller employers combined in associations to follow, as convenient, a policy of peace or war with the organizations that sought to recruit their employees. In 1903 local organizations of employers, manufacturers' associations, industrial associations, employers' associations, and citizens' alliances joined forces to resist the demands of organized labor. They formed the Citizens' Industrial Association, with David M. Parry of the National Association of Manufacturers as chairman of the executive committee. "Organized labor," he accused, ". . . does not place its reliance upon reason and justice, but on strikes, boycotts, and coercion. . . . It denies to those outside its ranks the individual right to dispose of their labor as they see fit—a right that is one of the most sacred and fundamental of American liberty."

The Citizens' Industrial Association sought "to establish and maintain industrial peace, and to create and direct a public sentiment in opposition to all forms of violence, coercion and intimidation." It urged employers to organize to forestall the spread of unionism. Under the leadership of C. W. Post, a wealthy dry cereal manufacturer, the Citizens' Industrial Association carried on propaganda through public meetings and in paid advertisements. In some communities, the citizens' alliances resorted to stronger tactics.

The citizens' alliances were a factor in the Colorado mining wars of 1903 and 1904. Cripple Creek, a union stronghold, was the center of the dispute. Although relations between the miners and the operators had been peaceful for more than a decade, the representatives of the State miners' association had declared that one of their purposes was "to fight . . . the miners' unions of the state." Thus began a contest of unparalleled violence between the Western Federation of Miners and the operators, which resulted in the virtual ousting of the union from the Colorado mining camps.

The union struck the mines at Idaho Springs and the smelters of the American Smelting and Refining Company at Denver. A strike of mill men for reduction of hours was going on simultaneously in Telluride. At Cripple Creek sporadic violence flared. Pleas were made to Governor James H. Peabody by the mine owners for troops; petitions not to intervene arrived from union supporters.

The Governor's investigating team recommended sending troops. They arrived under the command of General Sherman M. Bell, who directed a reign of terror against the strikers. Unionists retaliated by

blowing up a mine and killing two men, then dynamiting the Independence station, which took the lives
of thirteen nonunion miners.

Union men were arrested and herded into the "bull
pen," a cattle stockyard. The cooperative stores
owned by the union were sacked and their contents
stolen or thrown out and burned. Leaders were imprisoned. Lawyers sought their release, but the majority of the Colorado Supreme Court supported the detention under the Governor's proclamation of martial
law. Members of the Western Federation of Miners
were driven out of the district. When the Governor
was asked by the *New York World* whether it was
true that destitute miners were being deported to
Kansas, he replied that "rioting, dynamiting and anarchy has had its day in Colorado."

On December 30, 1905, the ex-governor of Idaho,
Frank Steunberg, was murdered. A man named Harry
Orchard confessed the deed, but he claimed that the
Western Federation of Miners' leaders, William "Big
Bill" Haywood, Charles Moyer, and Denver businessman George A. Pettibone, put him up to it. He said
their motive was revenge on the Governor who,
elected with labor support, called out the troops in
the Coeur d'Alene strike of 1899. Idaho officials kidnapped the accused in Denver and took them across
the state line for trial. The prosecution was directed by
the famous William Borah, but he was to meet his
match in the defense attorney Clarence Darrow, who
skillfully convinced a specially picked "hanging Jury"
to acquit the accused.

The mine owners' campaign destroyed the Western

Federation of Miners throughout virtually all of the metalliferous mining areas of Colorado. Weakened by the ordeal the organization became a prey to internal bickering. There was not much the union could do except to defend itself, but it was not equal to the massed might of the mine operators supported by the citizens' alliances and the government.

Over the years the United Mine Workers of America had attempted to organize the Colorado coal fields, but to no avail. The companies, led by the Rockefeller-owned Colorado Fuel and Iron Company, would not deal with the union. These companies dominated the Colorado mining areas "through the ruthless suppression of unionism, accomplished by the use of the power of summary discharge, the black list, armed guards, and spies, and by the active aid of venal state, county and town officials."

Seeking union recognition, the miners wanted wages of $3.45 a day, the eight-hour day, a union man checking the weighing of coal (for they felt the company was cheating them), the right not to buy at the company store, and the "abolition of the notorious and criminal guard system which has prevailed in the mining camps of Colorado for many years." The operators refused. In September, 1913, the miners voted to strike. Sheriff Jefferson Farr of Huerfano County immediately commissioned several hundred deputies.

Workers left company-owned hovels for tent camps in Ludlow and nearby areas established by the UMW. In the meantime, the Colorado Fuel and Iron Company provided its guards with a specially built armored car, the "Death Special," which could be used to intimidate pickets and strikers. The miners began to arm after several of their number were killed. Clashes between strikers and guards increased.

Yielding to the companies' pressure, Governor Elias Ammons sent the National Guard into the strike district. At first the strikers welcomed the soldiers, who had been instructed to protect property and preserve the peace. But when the militiamen sided with the company guards and deputies, the miners protested. Subsequently the governor withdrew most of the National Guard, leaving a company commanded by Lieutenant Karl E. Linderfelt, a "rare combination of a bully and a bulldog."

On April 20, 1914, Ludlow exploded. Linderfelt's soldiers attacked the tent colony, spraying it with bullets and setting fire to the tents. Eleven children and two women died in the flames. Louis Tikas, strike leader at Ludlow, and two others were murdered. Angered miners burned mines and killed guardsmen. The military began falling back as strikers advanced to the cry "Remember Ludlow!" In a ten-day war, forty-six people died in the assault, most of them company guards.

President Woodrow Wilson, at the request of the governor, sent in federal troops, and it was all over. Court-martials absolved soldiers of any responsibility in the Ludlow Massacre. Linderfelt, tried for murder, got off with a light reprimand.

The mining wars in the Rocky Mountain states had their eastern counterpart in West Virginia, where the United Mine Workers embarked on a major organizing effort in 1912. The union demanded wage increases, the eight-hour day, the checkoff, and no discrimination for union membership. The companies refused. A strike was called on April 20.

Guards supplied by the Baldwin-Felts agency and three companies of National Guardsmen were sent to the scene. The officer in charge "proceeded on the theory that a state of war existed, there, and we were exercising war powers." On February 7, 1913, an armored train, the "Bull Moose" special, attacked the miners' tent colony at Holly Grove. Armed men fired more than 200 shots into the sleeping village. Quin Morton, general manager of Imperial Coal Company, boasted: "We will go back and give them another round." When testifying before a committee of the U.S. Senate, Morton was asked whether "a cultured gentleman approves of the use of a machine gun in a populous village." One senator called Morton's conduct "appalling, horrible." The strike ended in April, 1913, with the companies promising not to discriminate against union members, a promise broken.

The anthracite fields of Pennsylvania had also been bloodied when miners challenged the superior might of the coal operators. In 1900 the United Mine Workers of America had called its first strike in these fields. It lasted a little over a month. According to UMW President John Mitchell, the anthracite strike of 1900 "stands out in bold relief as the most remarkable contest between labor and capital in the industrial history of our nation; remarkable because it involved a greater number of persons than any other industrial contest; because of the entire absence of lawlessness on the part of those who engaged in the strike; and

last, but not least, because it was the only great contest in which the workers came out entirely and absolutely victorious."

While the last part of Mitchell's statement was
more than a slight exaggeration, the outcome of the
strike was a solid victory for the union. A more serious encounter began in May, 1902, and lasted until
mid-October. From the beginning the strike had been
a violent one. Shootings, killings, and attacks upon
the colliers were frequent. In the midst of the strike,
George F. Baer, head of the Reading Railroad and
spokesman for the mine operators, penned his famous
"divine right" letters. When a Wilkes-Barre photog-
rapher appealed to him on the basis of Christian
principles to settle the strike, Baer replied:

"I do not know who you are. I see that you are a
Christian man; but you are evidently biased in favor
of the right of the working man to control a business
in which he has no interest other than to secure fair
wages for the work he does. I beg of you not to be
discouraged. The right and interests of the laboring
man will be protected and cared for—not by the labor
agitators, but by the Christian men to whom God in
his infinite wisdom has given the control of the property interests of the country, and upon the successful
Management of which so much depends. Do not be
discouraged. Pray earnestly that right may triumph,
always remembering that the Lord God Omnipotent
still reigns, and that His reign is one of law and order,
and not of violence and crime."

Dominated by such sentiments, the coal operators
would accept no compromise. Baer criticized Presi-

dent Theodore Roosevelt for urging a settlement with "fomentors . . . of anarchy." Roosevelt later confided that he would like to have taken Baer "by the seat of the breeches and the nape of the neck and chucked him out of the window."

Only after an appeal to J. P. Morgan, the dominant investment banker of the time, did the operators agree to arbitration by a Presidential commission. The union was anxious to have a labor man on the panel. Roosevelt "sneaked" E. E. Clark, Grand Chief of the Order of Conductors, on the commission as an "eminent sociologist." The award of the commission did not grant as much as the union expected, but it included a ten percent increase in wages and a reduction in hours of work. In addition, the use of private guards was held to be against the public interest. The commission did not recommend the recognition of the union, but it did agree that differences between the employer and his employees should "first be considered in conference between the operator or his official representative, and a committee chosen by his employees from their own ranks." While the issue of child labor was not directly submitted, the commission deplored the employment of male children as breaker boys, and noted that the statutory age of employment was not sufficiently high.

"The story of coal is always the same," wrote Mary "Mother" Jones, self-styled "hell raiser" and a devoted fighter for the rights of miners to form a union. "It is a dark story. For a second's more sunlight, men must fight like tigers. For the privilege of seeing the color of their children's eyes by the light of the sun, fathers must fight as beasts in the jungle. That life may have something of decency, something of beauty—a picture, a new dress, a bit of cheap lace fluttering in the window—for this, men who work down in the mines must struggle and lose, struggle and win."

The victory in the anthracite fields was one of the greatest in American labor history. It was gained against the formidable opposition of the operators in an industry dominated by the same financial groups which sought to limit the influence of unionisn in other industries. By willingness to accept less than their demands, the mine workers, under the leadership of Mitchell, were able to force open a door to labor organizations that had been closed since the demise of the Workingmen's Benevolent Association in the early 1870s.

Employers have in disputes with their employees utilized the legal weapons that were available. By the turn of the century the use of the labor injunction was already established. It was a method by which equity courts forbade picketing or other union activities during a labor dispute. It was also used to prohibit the boycott of a good or service of an "unfair" employer. The injunction was effective because those refusing to obey the order of a court could be adjudged in contempt and sentenced to a fine or imprisonment.

Legislation to limit the writ of injunction had been introduced in Congress in 1900, but no action was taken. Before the end of the decade the unions faced another serious problem, the liability of an organization of labor under the Sherman Antitrust law for damages incurred by an employer as a result of a secondary boycott. The United Hatters of North America, as a result of a dispute with D. E. Loewe & Co., a manufacturer of men's hats in Danbury, Connecticut, instituted a nationwide boycott. Unionists from all over the country urged dealers not to handle Loewe merchandise. Advertisements sponsored by the United Hatters asked readers to forego Loewe products. Loewe warned the members of the Hatters' Union that their conduct was illegal. When the union ignored the warning, Loewe sued.

The case was in the courts for twelve years. In 1908, the Supreme Court held that any combination which "obstructs the free flow of commerce or restricts in that regard the liberty of a trader to engage in business" may have violated the antitrust laws. The case was brought to trial and the union found guilty. The decision was unexpected, and it was believed that the labor unions would be flooded by suits charging violations of the Sherman laws and that verdicts of triple damages would bankrupt the union treasuries and jeopardize the savings of the members.

While the Danbury Hatters' case was going through the courts, an attack upon the boycott was made by James Van Cleave, owner of the Buck's Stove and Range Company and a leader of the militant anti-unionists. A strike had been called at Van Cleave's factory, and its products placed on the unfair list by the AFL, a fact regularly announced by the *American Federationist,* the AFL's official journal. Van Cleave secured an order from the District of Columbia federal court directing the removal of the offensive announcement. Considering that the court order violated the first amendment, Gompers refused to obey. He and Frank Morrison, secretary of the AFL, and John Mitchell, a vice-president, were adjudged guilty of contempt of court and sentenced to jail.

While the case was passing through the courts, Van Cleave died and his successor settled with the unions. The court upheld the injunction, but the jail sentences were set aside. The trial judge then appointed a prosecuting committee and again found the defendants guilty of contempt. However, the Supreme Court ruled that the statute of limitations barred punishment.

The attack upon the boycott, the utilization of the injunction in labor disputes by the courts, and the unresponsiveness of Congress to the AFL's appeals for remedial legislation caused the AFL to become more active in the national political arena. To show its displeasure at the failure of Congress, delegates from fifty-one unions assembled in Washington in March, 1906, and drew up a "Bill of Grievances." Congress was charged with failing to deal adequately with the competition of convict labor, immigration, the granting of equal rights to seamen. In addition, Congress had refused to protect the right of federal employees to petition for redress, relieve unions from the threat of prosecution under the antitrust laws, or to limit the right of the courts to issue injunctions in labor disputes.

Although the AFL was the predominant labor organization, radicals had been trying to "capture" the trade unions since the 1890s. The Western Federation of Miners had become disenchanted with the AFL's conservative outlook and helped establish successively the Western Labor Union and the American Labor

Union. In the eastern part of the country, the Socialist Trade and Labor Alliance was formed by adherents of the Socialist Labor Party.

In 1905, a successful attempt was made to unite the separate independent groups into one organization. A group of leaders who believed another federation of labor espousing a more radical doctrine was needed met in Chicago "to confederate the workers of this country into a working class movement that shall have for its purpose that emancipation of the working class . . . having in view no compromise and no surrender." Thus was launched the Industrial Workers of the World. The Wobblies, as members called themselves, advocated the abolition of capitalism and the formation of industrial unions.

Presiding at the convention was William D. Haywood, head of the Western Federation of Miners. He proclaimed that "we are going down in the gutter to get the mass of workers and bring them up to a decent plane of living." Despite ringing oratory and rousing songs, it was obvious that the IWW did not have a ready formula for success. Conflicting elements could not live together in the same organization. At the second IWW convention, the trade unionists with the most industrial experience, including the Western Federation of Miners, withdrew. At the fourth convention, in 1908, the followers of the Socialist Labor Party left or were driven out. As a result of these secessions, the IWW became an organization of migratory workers with an anarcho-syndicalist orientation. For the next few years it devoted itself to carrying on free-speech fights in the West. Though revolution was the final aim, the present need, in the words of one IWW official, was "a bed to sleep in, water enough to take a bath in and decent food to eat."

In the East, the IWW turned its attention to steelworkers in McKees Rocks, Pennsylvania, and textile workers in Lawrence, Massachusetts; Paterson, New Jersey; and Little Falls, New York. The Lawrence strike was a dramatic struggle by thousands of workers, many of them of foreign origin, but it led to no permanent organization. The ability of the IWW leaders to mobilize large unskilled masses to display their poverty and suffering was of a high order, but they failed in the elementary ability needed to build a permanent organization.

When the United States entered World War I, Wobblies by the hundreds were rounded up and sent to jail. Accused of hampering the war effort, they became targets of vigilante groups who sometimes took the law into their own hands. It is true that the IWW had traditionally opposed war; its 1916 convention condemned "all wars and, for the prevention of such, we proclaim the anti-militarist propaganda in time of peace, thus promoting Class Solidarity among the workers of the entire world, and, in time of war, the General Strike in all industries."

Socialist leader Eugene Debs openly spoke out against the war. Indicted for violating the Espionage Act, he said at his trial: "Years ago I recognized my kinship with all living things, and I made up my mind that I was not one bit better than the meanest on earth. I said then, and I say now, that while there is a lower class, I am in it, while there is a criminal element, I am of it, and while there is a soul in prison, I am not free." Debs was found guilty.

He had been converted to socialism while in jail for his role as leader of the Pullman strike. Running for President of the United States in 1912, he polled nearly a million votes. A born agitator. Debs told working people: "Intelligent discontent is the mainspring of civilization. It is agitation or stagnation. I have taken my choice." Individual status and power seeking was for the small in soul. Debs chose to remain with the rank and file. Hoosier poet James Whitcomb Riley said of him:

> *As warm a heart as ever beat*
> *Betwixt here and the judgment seat.*

Critics called Debs a perpetual failure, traveling from defeat to defeat. He might have said, as did socialist leader Norman Thomas, that he fought not for lost causes but causes yet to be won.

Socialists had comparatively more influence within the labor movement than in the country at large. They were active in many unions, and some occupied high office. For many years, Max Hayes, a member of the International Typographical Union, was the leading socialist spokesman on the floor of the AFL convention. In 1912, he ran for president of the AFL, receiving almost half as many votes as Gompers.

The socialists were concerned with promoting the policy of an independent labor party. Many also supported reform of the AFL's structure so that a number of the crafts would combine into industrial unions. But the socialists' influence was short-lived. Their antiwar stance in 1917 and the emergence of communists in their ranks proved self-destructive.

Meanwhile AFL leaders were pledging "ourselves in peace and in war, in stress or in storm, to stand unreservedly by the standards of liberty and the safety and preservation of the institutions and ideals of our Republic." The most important addition to the ranks of organized labor between 1900 and World War I was the clothing industries. The battle for recognition began in New York City, the major market for women's clothing, where the International Ladies Garment Workers Union struggled to survive. Conditions in the industry were deplorable. Low wages, long hours, and unsanitary and unsafe working places were commonplace.

In March, 1911, a fire at the Triangle Shirtwaist Company claimed the lives of 148 employees, most of them young women. As flames spread throughout the eighth floor, workers jumped to their deaths. Scores of charred bodies were found piled against closed doors. They had been kept bolted, a newspaper reported, "to safeguard employers from the loss of goods by the departure of workers . . ." From the ashes of this disaster sprang the movement for industrial safety with the passage of factory inspection laws.

Garment workers revolted at inhumane conditions occasionally and went out on strike. But once grievances were temporarily eliminated, there would be an exodus from the union. This tendency continued for twenty years, and some believed that Jewish workers would never be able to form stable labor unions.

The theory was weakened in 1909 when 30,000 striking waistmakers, seventy percent of them women, heard Gompers ask them "to stand together, to have faith in yourselves, to be true to your comrades . . . Let your watchword be: Union and progress, and until then, no surrender." The strike was an eye-opener to those who doubted the stamina of garment workers. For fourteen weeks the picket lines held. and the strikers gained contracts in 354 shops.

That was only a curtain raiser. The next summer 60,000 cloakmakers struck for a pay raise and the closed union shop. Strikers held the picket lines until a favorable settlement was reached on September 16. The following week began a struggle for the unionization of the men's garment trades in Chicago. A foreman in one of the Hart, Schaffner and Marx plants reduced piece rates, a practice normally accepted without protest. However, this time it was rejected, and the incident sparked a major revolt. The United Garment Workers of America called a general strike, and 41,000 workers responded. They gained a costly and limited victory. The strike lasted 133 days, $200,000 was paid out for relief, hundreds of workers were arrested, and seven were killed.

Both the United Garment Workers and the International Ladies Garment Workers Union were made up of predominantly Jewish and Italian immigrants, although the national leadership of the United Garment Workers was predominantly native born. At the convention of the United Garment Workers in 1914, a conflict between the two groups resulted in the formation of the Amalgamated Clothing Workers of

America, which became the dominant organization in the men's clothing industry.

Immigration policy was one of the issues that divided the leaders of labor. Virtually all unionists favored exclusion of Orientals and believed that the limitless flow of immigrants to the United States tended to depress wages. Between 1903 and 1914 more than 800,000 immigrants entered the United States annually, with a peak of 1,387,318 in 1913.

The issue of immigration exclusion was debated at AFL conventions and at the 1910 convention of the Socialist Party. The majority of the Socialist convention's committee on immigration recommended limiting the number. Milwaukee's Victor L. Berger, elected that year as the first Congressman chosen on the Socialist ticket, spoke in favor of the restrictive proposal. An immigrant himself, he reasoned: "Now I believe in the motto of Marx that the proletarians of all countries should unite, absolutely. But he [Marx] did not say, nor would he say if they should unite in Milwaukee, Chicago or New York." Adolph Germer, a coal miner destined to be a future leader of the CIO, complained that many foreigners acted as strikebreakers and were not reliable for the long pull.

The American Federation of Labor for a time opposed outright restrictions upon immigration. But in the early years of the century it favored an educational test and, after World War I, endorsed the quota system for limiting entry. Restrictions upon Chinese immigration were endorsed from the beginning. It was the adverse influence of the immigrant upon the labor market rather than opposition based on race or religion which accounted for the negative attitude of organized labor. That's why the AFL supported the quota laws of 1921 and 1924 which limited immigration to a percentage of nationals living in the United States. The law of 1924 was attacked as favoring immigrants from northern Europe at the expense of those from Italy and the Slavic nations, but to organized labor these measures represented the means to restrict the continual flow of immigration.

World War I reduced immigration to the United States to a trickle. Recruiting agents from northern industries found substitutes among southern blacks. Between 1916 and 1924, hundreds of thousands streamed north to the automobile, meat packing, iron and steel, and railroad industries. Most of the black workers filled semiskilled and unskilled jobs.

The influx of thousands of black workers into northern industrial areas created many problems for the new arrivals. Coming largely from rural areas and having virtually no knowledge of union organizations, they were more susceptible to strikebreaking than white workers. The employment of large numbers of black strikebreakers in the wave of post-World War I labor disputes exacerbated the feeling of hostility between the races. An estimated 30,000 black strikebreakers worked in the 1919 steel strike. Labor leader John Fitzpatrick feared that if this continued, the industrial centers "are bound to be paralyzed by race riots . . . As I find it the Northern Negro is alive to the situation and cannot be used to any great extent, but the Southern Negro is brutally exploited and has no real knowledge of the situation in which he is being used."

While Northerners were debating what to do with the black workers, they were welcomed by the Alabama labor movement. When the unions of the state established the Alabama State Federation of Labor, in 1901, they elected two blacks as vice-presidents.

The quality of the Alabama unionists was revealed at the 1902 convention held in Selma. Vice-President J.H. Beane, a black man, informed newspapers: "The State Federation does not draw the color line, and the delegates will be seated as in all general conventions under the American Federation of Labor . . . Color or creed is no bar to a fair day's service. If the people of Selma for this reason turn the cold shoulder to the Alabama State Federation of Labor in the matter of hall accommodations it will not in any way interfere with the deliberations of the convention."

Blacks and whites cooperated on the picket line in strikes in the mines and plants where both races were employed. A considerable increase in the employment of black workers took place on the railroads during the strike of shopmen in 1922. The six railway shopcrafts agreed with the AFL Executive Council that black mechanics, helpers, and laborers would be allowed to become members of the International Brotherhood of Firemen and Oilers. A small group of black employees of the Pullman Company established the Brotherhood of Sleeping Car Porters in New York City on August 25, 1925. A. Philip Randolph was invited to address the group, and he became its first organizer.

In Randolph, the Porters' Union selected a man of unusual eloquence, one who was to devote almost forty years to eliminating discrimination by unions against black workers.

The struggle for the eight-hour day was initiated by the four major operating crafts on the railroads. When negotiations proved unsuccessful, the four railroad brotherhoods took the unprecedented step of scheduling a nationwide railroad strike to begin on September 4, 1916. On September 2, President Wilson addressed a joint session of Congress and appealed for the enactment of an eight-hour law to govern railroad operations. Congress acted quickly, and a bill was in his hands on September 3. He signed it the day before the strike date. The brotherhoods knew that the law would be challenged in the courts, and demanded the eight-hour day be put in effect on January 1, 1917. Once war was declared, the union leaders were convinced it would not be possible to seek a solution through a strike.

Three members of the Council of National Defense, including Gompers, were dispatched by President Wilson to meet the head of the railroad unions and seek a peaceful solution. They agreed to the eight-hour work schedule a day before the Supreme Court found the law constitutional.

In December, 1917, the federal government took over the operation of the railroads. No discrimination for union membership was allowed, and wages were set by a government board. Despite the liberal labor policies followed, discontent among workers mounted as the war went on. In 1917, strikes reached the highest level in history, 4,450.

In an effort to deal with the problem, President Woodrow Wilson created the National War Labor Board, made up of an equal number of employer and union representatives. The Board agreed there should be no strikes or lockouts during the war, and that workers were to have the right to organize into unions of their choosing for purposes of collective bargaining. Employers were to have the right to organize associations. Workers were not to be discharged for belonging or being active in trade unions, but they were to refrain from coercive methods in recruiting members or seeking bargaining rights. In the sixteen months it functioned, the Board disposed of more than 1,100 cases.

Union membership rose substantially during the war years; in transportation it virtually doubled. The metal and building trades also gained, as did unions on the docks and on the ships. With the end of the war, the organized labor movement faced a number of problems requiring almost immediate solutions. The increased memberships in many unions were impatient with cautious traditional tactics. A search for new policies and methods was under way. The belief that the heads of the movement were old and weary and that individual unions as well as the general labor movement were in need of new and more imaginative leadership was widespread.

Business leaders were also unhappy about the course of events during the war. In their view, organized labor had become too strong; its improved bargaining position and the protection of the government had allowed unions to expand and gain a foothold in industries normally opposed to their recognition. Labor's more aggressive opponents urged business to organize so as to resist any further encroachments upon the rights of management. As a consequence, the immediate postwar period witnessed an epidemic of labor disputes.

The first manifestation of the new-found militancy was the Seattle general strike, called in support of the striking metal trades workers in the shipyards. Food kitchens and milk stations were set up, and the people went about their affairs with few protests and little difficulty. The city's crime rate actually was below normal in this period.

On the second day of the strike, Mayor Ole Hanson issued a proclamation in which he guaranteed the people of Seattle "absolute and complete protection . . . . The anarchists in the community shall not rule its affairs. All persons violating the laws will be dealt with summarily." The strike, which accomplished little, lasted five days.

More unusual was the strike of the Boston Police. When a plan for adjusting wages and working conditions had failed, the policemen struck on September 11, 1919. Absence of police was followed by twenty-four hours of rioting, looting, and violence. At the request of the city authorities, Governor Calvin Coolidge sent 5,000 militiamen to keep order. "There is no right to strike against the public safety by anybody, anywhere, anytime," he declared. Clashes between roving mobs and soldiers resulted in the killing of eight civilians. By September 14, the strike was virtually over. Coolidge, who had denounced the strike as a "desertion of duty," became a national hero.

Despite reversals, the labor movement expanded at a greater rate than ever. Almost one million additional members joined the unions in 1919. Actors, after a strike lasting a month, won recognition for the newly organized Actors Equity Association. The first contract specified the number of performances a week that could be required without payment of overtime, limited rehearsal time, and required arbitration of unsettled differences.

In May, 1920, the United Mine Workers mustered an "army" to move into the nonunion counties of McDowell, Mingo, and Logan, West Virginia. In one shootout eight men and a boy were killed. Repeated skirmishes brought federal toops into the area; finally the miners were peaceably disarmed and dispersed. The union failed in its campaign.

After the expulsion of the Amalgamated Association of Iron, Steel and Tin Workers from the plants of the U.S. Steel Corporation, the absence of a strong union in the steel industry was regarded as a sign of a weak labor movement. In 1918, the AFL convention endorsed a joint campaign by the twenty-four unions having jurisdiction in the steel industry. The campaign was one of the more successful in labor history. Thousands of steelworkers joined unions.

More difficult was obtaining industry recognition. Elbert Gary, board chairman of U.S. Steel Corporation, refused to meet a union committee to discuss the matter. A strike called for September 22, 1919, was answered by 367,000 steelworkers.

Confrontations between strikers, private guards, and the local police began immediately. Local officials suppressed strike meetings. The mayor of Duquesne, Pennsylvania, justified his denial of a speaking permit to AFL Secretary Frank Morrison by saying: "Jesus Christ himself could not speak in Duquesne." Throughout the strike Gary maintained his imperturbability and reiterated his view that U.S. Steel did not deal with unions. During the strike, one of the bloodier of the time, twenty people, eighteen of them strikers, were killed. U.S. Steel had triumphed and would remain the bastion of the open shop for another seventeen years.

In the midst of the strike, President Wilson convened an industrial conference with representatives from business, labor, and the public. The main purpose of the conference was to work out methods that would promote industrial peace. As a minimum the labor delegates wanted the conference to recognize the right of employees to bargain through outside unions, but the employer group would only accept collective bargaining through company-controlled organizations.

Company unions of various sorts had developed early in the century and had multiplied during the war. Large employers also developed paternalistic welfare plans under which they aided home ownership by their employees through supporting low mortgage rates, subsidized lunches, encouraged savings, and established profit-sharing plans. Systems of grievance procedure through which employee complaints could be considered were organized, but the employer generally held the right to make the final decision. The programs were primarily designed to eliminate the influence of the outside union on the work force.

A more extensive campaign for eliminating the influence of unions in industry was the American Plan of Employment which promoted the open shop. The program had considerable success, and established systems of collective bargaining. as in the Chicago and the San Francisco building trades, buckled under the attack of the open shop contractors.

At one time twenty-two states had laws making it a criminal offense for employers to discharge union members or to deny employment because of membership in a union. The federal government incorporated such a provision in the Erdman Act of 1898 regulating the railroads. But in a case involving the right of the federal government to enforce the prohibition against discrimination of railroad employees, the Supreme Court held that workers could be discharged for any reason, including membership in a labor union. In the Kansas statute forbidding discrimination for union membership, the Court held that an employer could not be penalized for compelling one of his employees to give up his union membership.

These decisions removed any legislative protection that union members may have enjoyed against discrimination. In another case the Supreme Court ruled against attempts to unionize employees who had signed a "yellow-dog contract," an agreement under which the prospective employee agreed not to join a union during his tenure with the employer. The National War Labor Board had directed employers to abandon such contracts, but they increased greatly after the end of World War I, and were used to block organizing throughout the nonunion areas of West Virginia. They were also used by employers who would hire professional strikebreakers and have them sign an agreement not to join a union.

Inability to obtain relief from Congress turned many sections of organized labor towards independent political action. By 1922, the proponents met and organized the Conference for Progressive Political Action, which was dominated by the railroad unions, although socialists and traditional supporters of an independent labor party were allowed admission; the communists were excluded. Groups speaking for the new body endorsed some congressional candidates in 1922, and when the presidential nominees of the Democratic and the Republican parties did not meet their criteria for endorsement, they nominated Robert M. LaFollette for president and Burton K. Wheeler for vice-president. The AFL endorsed the ticket. Considering the absence of organizational support outside of Wisconsin, La Follette's home state, the third party candidates did very well. However, the railway unions, concerned with their positions in the Congress and the state legislatures, backed out of the alliance.

The antiunion open-shop campaigns seriously affected membership. From 1920 to 1923, it declined from 5,047,800 to 3,622,000.

Congress made a giant step forward in providing protection against discrimination for union membership when it enacted the Railway Labor Act of 1926. Section two allowed each side to designate representatives for purposes of collective bargaining without interference from the other. In addition a board of mediation was set up to aid the parties to reach an agreement. In the event of a shutdown of rail service which might affect the public interest, the law provided for the appointment of an emergency board of inquiry by the President.

The power of Congress to outlaw discriminatory labor practices was upheld by a unanimous Supreme Court. A railroad company had interfered with the right of its employees to self-organization, and the Brotherhood of Railway Clerks sued. It was ordered to (1) disestablish the company union, (2) reinstate the Brotherhood as the representative of the employees until a choice by secret ballot is made, (3) reinstate employees who had been discharged for activity in the Brotherhood. Mr. Chief Justice Hughes, who wrote the unanimous opinion for the Court, said that the workers' right to organize "to safeguard their proper interests is not to be disputed . . . . Congress was not required to ignore this right of the employees but could safeguard it and seek to make their appropriate collective action an instrument of peace rather than of strike." He denied that the law would limit the right of the employer to hire or discharge employees. "The statute is not aimed at the right of the employers but interference with the freedom of the employees to have representatives of their own choosing. As the carriers subject to the Act have no constitutional right to interfere with the freedom of the employees in making their selection they cannot complain of the statute on constitutional grounds."

The 1920s witnessed the gradual reduction of the

power of the United Mine Workers. In 1922, half a million soft-coal miners and 150,000 anthracite miners joined in a massive strike. Secretary of Commerce Herbert Hoover ruled out federal intervention, declaring: "The government's position has long been known to be that sooner or later there would have to be a showdown in the mine fields. Its attitude is that if a strike must be, it must be, and the sooner the issue is disposed of the better."

As operators engaged in cutthroat competition, John L. Lewis, president of the UMW, thundered "no backward step," which meant no downward wage adjustment. The policy of "no backward step" proved to be no solution. Although compromises were worked out with operators in Illinois and other fields, the miners decided to resist in Ohio and western Pennsylvania. The strike began in the summer of 1927. It was a bitter and heart-rending struggle, with famished families evicted from their homes. In July, 1928, the union admitted defeat.

Ominously, a report from the AFL research department in February, 1928, called attention to increasing unemployment among organized workers. Neither the Labor Department nor the Government was prepared for the catastrophe which followed. In May, 1929, the executive council of the AFL suggested the establishment of a national employment service, a census to determine the number of unemployed, and regularization of employment. In November, a month after the stock market crash, President Hoover asked industry to avoid wage cuts and to speed investment.

The absence of relief and welfare' systems deprived

millions of the bare necessities. Dire want forced them to seek assistance for themselves and their families, but none was available. State and local governments made some efforts to provide relief, until their budgets were exhausted. Pleas for federal aid were rejected by President Herbert Hoover, who insisted that the nation had "turned the corner." The attempts of Congress to provide aid were vetoed as a threat to the credit of the federal government.

With business depressed and its promises of permanent prosperity a bitter memory, Congress enacted the Norris-LaGuardia Act. The law deprived the federal courts of the power to prohibit certain types of union activity, organization, assembly, strikes, picketing, and collective acts which can be performed by an individual. The yellow-dog contract was declared against public policy.

The labor movement survived the Great Depression shaken but intact. With the advent of the New Deal, its unions were to initiate the greatest organizing drives in history.

California workers ride to rebellion against the "rich farmer." Library of Congress.

★ 5 ★

AMERICANS IN
DEPRESSION AND WAR

by Irving Bernstein

Unemployment was the overriding fact of life when Franklin D. Roosevelt became President of the United States on March 4, 1933. An anomaly of the time was that the government did not systematically collect statistics on joblessness, actually did not start doing so until 1940. The Bureau of Labor Statistics later estimated that 12,830,000 persons were out of work in 1933, about one-fourth of a civilian labor force of over fifty-one million. March was the record month, with about fifteen and a half million unemployed. There is no doubt that 1933 was the worst year, and March the worst month for joblessness in the history of the United States.

But there was another side to the problem. Following the stock market crash of 1929, the Hoover Administration urged—and many industries and unions adopted—work-sharing. For example, the United States Steel Corporation in 1929 had 224,980 full-time employees. The number shrank to 211,055 in 1930, to 53,619 in 1931, to 18,938 in 1932, and to zero on April 1, 1933. All who remained on the payroll on this last date were part time, and they were only half as numerous as those on full time in 1929.

Massive unemployment had a profound social and emotional impact upon American workers and their families. The movement of population, historically a response to economic opportunity, changed drastically when opportunity dried up. Immigration from abroad virtually stopped. The long-term shift from farm to city slowed significantly and there was, in fact, some reverse migration. The great population movement of the thirties was transiency—the worker adrift in a sea of unemployment. People, especially the young, girls as well as boys, took to the road because they could no longer bear to stay home. In the middle of the decade when the dust blew in the Great Plains, wiping out their farms, whole families of Okies, Arkies, and Mizoos migrated west, especially to California. The migrants often made their way to the junk-pile Hoovervilles with their Prosperity Roads, Hard Times Avenues, and Easy Streets. The destitute often lost their homes or farms because they were unable to make payments on mortgages.

When Roosevelt became President one of his most urgent tasks was to devise a new federal relief policy. Historically, private charity and local government had cared for the indigent. Both soon exhausted their resources, and the states, starting with New York in 1931 when Roosevelt was governor, stepped in. Frances Perkins, his Industrial Commissioner, was charged with the enforcement of labor laws. She was appointed Secretary of Labor after Roosevelt took office, the first time a woman was named to the Cabinet.

Roosevelt signed the Federal Emergency Relief Act on May 12, 1933. The President selected Harry L.

Hopkins, who had headed the New York relief program, to run FERA. A gifted administrator, Hopkins quickly put the program into high gear. He gathered a small staff in Washington and brought the state relief organizations into the FERA system. While the agency tried to provide all the necessities, food came first. City dwellers usually got an allowance for fuel, and rent for one month was provided in case of eviction. FERA paid for medicine, some doctor bills, but no hospital costs. Work relief sewing rooms renovated hand-me-down clothing. One of the most significant FERA policies was to grant relief without discrimination. Blacks, especially in the South, who had never before gotten anything from government, suddenly found themselves eligible for federal relief and moved onto the rolls.

During the spring of 1933, Roosevelt launched two programs to revive business and increase employment. The National Recovery Administration, under General Hugh S. Johnson, allowed businessmen to fix prices and allocate production quotas through codes of "fair competition," and without regard to the anti-trust laws. The codes also set minimum wages and maximum hours of employment. The Public Works Administration, under Secretary of the Interior Harold L. Ickes, constructed major capital improvements.

Employment effects of both programs were disappointing. An NRA "boomlet" during the summer petered out in September. PWA projects were inherently long term, for example, building the Grand Coulee Dam on the Columbia River and the Triborough Bridge in New York City; and Ickes insisted on careful planning and the avoidance of graft, which caused delay. Roosevelt and Hopkins feared that the jobless would suffer cruelly during the winter of 1933-34, as they had the previous year. Thus, in the fall of 1933, Hopkins urged and the President accepted a proposal for a forced draft work relief program, called the Civil Works Administration. PWA transferred funds to CWA. In effect, FERA turned itself into CWA, and by December 15, Hopkins had four million people at work on secondary roads, schoolhouses, playgrounds, parks, among many other projects. Most were welcomed by the communities that benefited, but some were hastily conceived and condemned as "leaf-raking." Significantly, millions of jobless workers got their families through a tough winter by earning wages for work performed. As CWA tapered off in the spring of 1934, FERA took over but now with a heavier emphasis on work relief.

Roosevelt, intensely interested in conservation, created a special relief program—the Civilian Conservation Corps—for young men to work in the forests. There were two purposes: to put jobless youth to useful work and to restore the land. The administrative machinery appeared cumbersome, but worked efficiently. The Labor Department recruited the jobless men, who were from families on relief, were unmarried, and were between the ages of sixteen and twenty-five. Army reserve officers managed the camps, and the Forest Service and the National Park Service planned the projects. Since the labor movement at the outset had opposed the program as "militarizing" labor, the President named Robert Fechner, vice-president of the Machinists, to head CCC.

Congress passed the Civilian Conservation bill on March 31, 1933. By June, 1,300 camps were in operation. All told, two and a half million young men went through the program. They planted trees; dug reservoirs, fishponds, and diversion ditches; built dams, bridges, and fire towers; fought tree diseases; restored historic battlefields; cleared beaches and campgrounds. They performed numerous other tasks to improve and protect the nation's natural resources while at the same time they reclaimed themselves. Their health improved in the outdoors; boys who had never been out of urban slums in the East visited the national parks in the West; the unskilled were taught trades; and whites and blacks learned to live together. The CCC, to Roosevelt's surprise, proved universally popular.

Because the National Industrial Recovery Act would encourage businessmen to join collectively in their self-interest, the American Federation of Labor insisted—and the key legislator, Senator Robert F. Wagner of New York, and Roosevelt agreed—that similar support should extend to workers. Thus, Section 7(a) of the statute required that every code of fair competition must contain the following conditions:

(1)   That employees shall have the right to organize and bargain collectively through representatives of their own choosing, and shall be free from the interference, restraint, or coercion of employers of labor, or their agents, in the designation of such representatives or in self-organization or in other concerted activities for the purpose of collective bargaining or other mutual aid or protection;

(2)   That no employee and no one seeking employment

shall be required as a condition of employment to join any company union or to refrain from joining, organizing, or assisting a labor organization of his own choosing.

This general language appeared to provide legal protection of workers' rights to form and join free trade unions while denying employers the right to impose company unions—or employee representation plans as they were then known—upon the workers.

The labor movement had been weak in the twenties, and the suffering of the Great Depression had given workers a deep sense of grievance. Section 7(a) was the spark that kindled a smoldering militancy.

John L. Lewis, president of the United Mine Workers of America, the largest of the industrial unions, recognized the opportunity to advance labor's cause. His aspiration was to unionize the unorganized mass production industries—steel, automobiles, rubber, nonferrous metals, shipbuilding, electrical equipment, among others—industries which the craft union-dominated AFL had largely ignored. But first Lewis must rebuild the UMW base in coal. The union had lost the heart of the old Central Competitive Field, western Pennsylvania and Ohio, in the late twenties, had never organized the great Southern Appalachian Field, and had contested with rival unions in Illinois and West Virginia. Lewis launched a massive organizing drive in June, 1933. The miners responded immediately and almost unanimously.

A new structure of bargaining, the Appalachian Agreement, was signed with the operators of the commercial mines on September 21, 1933. It established the UMW virtually overnight as the biggest and strongest of American labor unions. The unfinished

task was to make agreements with the steel corporations for their "captive" mines, that is, coal operations
they owned. These companies, which strongly opposed
unions and feared that Lewis would use the captive
mines to organize the steel mills, declined to bargain,
imposed company unions, and for a while refused to
allow representation elections. This led to a strike and
presidential intervention. Elections were then held at
several of the captive mines, which the UMW won.
Lewis thereby drove a wedge into the antiunion wall
of the steel industry.

While not so dramatically as the miners, other older
unions also made significant gains. Strikes in 1933 by
Sidney Hillman's Amalgamated Clothing Workers
brought in 50,000 new members as well as forcing
higher wages and shorter hours in the men's clothing
industry. Similar campaigns by David Dubinsky's International Ladies' Garment Workers' Union enjoyed
even greater success in many women's garment
markets. Significantly, the UMW, the ACW, and the
ILGWU, essentially industrial unions, agreed that the
great task before the American labor movement was
the unionization of the mass production industries.

Section 7(a) spurred organization in these basic industries and sparked the formation of unions in new
areas. Editorial employees on newspapers, for example,
established the American Newspaper Guild, conducted
strikes, and won contracts with many publishers. Motion picture actors created Screen Actors Guild. Agricultural workers engaged in major strikes, especially
in California where communists were in control, but
few led to permanent unions.

Thus, the combination of labor's new militancy and

the refusal of many employers, especially the big corporations, to engage in collective bargaining caused a great increase in strikes in the summer of 1933, particularly over the issue of recognition. Although the statute did not provide for it, Roosevelt on August 5, established an informal National Labor Board to handle 7(a) disputes. The Board consisted of three prominent industrialists, three leading trade unionists, and Senator Wagner as chairman. Since NLB could not compel compliance with its decisions, it depended upon persuasion.

NLB's notable achievement was the "Reading Formula," which became a cornerstone of national labor policy. It was implemented after the Full-Fashioned Hosiery Workers launched an organizing drive in the stocking mills around Reading, Pennsylvania. The employers refused recognition, and 10,000 workers walked out. On August 10, 1933, the Board mediated a strike settlement which provided for NLB to conduct secret-ballot elections to determine representatives. The employers agreed to bargain with the union if it won majorities. Elections were held, the union was selected at most mills, and written agreements were negotiated. Here the representation election served as a substitute for the strike over recognition.

The Reading Formula proved useful in a number of other situations, particularly the captive mines. But several large firms, notably the Weirton Steel and Budd Manufacturing companies, refused to permit elections and successfully challenged the shaky authority of the Board in the courts. The issue came to a head in the spring of 1934. The automobile industry, which had resisted the nascent auto unions and formed company unions, persuaded Roosevelt to establish a special Automobile Labor Board which recognized company unions and placed the principle of proportional representation (each organization speaking only for its own members) over exclusive representation (the union receiving a majority negotiating for all the workers). NLB virtually collapsed.

Senator Wagner, persuaded that Section 7(a) and the NLB experience should be incorporated into a new permanent law with a board responsible for its administration, introduced such a bill into Congress in the spring of 1934. Industry opposed the measure vigorously. This division and rising conflict over unionization in the steel industry led Roosevelt to defer action on Wagner's bill; instead, he won from Congress a general authorization for the President to establish boards to deal with labor disputes. By executive orders he then created several industry boards, starting with steel, along with a successor to NLB called the National Labor Relations Board. At the same time, the railway unions persuaded Congress to amend the Railway Labor Act of 1926 to establish a system in transportation much like that Wagner had proposed.

While 1933 had seen a dramatic growth of unions and many serious strikes, 1934 witnessed an eruption. There were 1,856 stoppages that year, by far the largest number since World War I. Many were accompanied by violence, and four constituted social upheavals in the affected communities. A walkout of auto parts workers at the Electric Auto-Lite Company's plants in Toledo, Ohio, disrupted that city and, in the face of the threat of a general strike, led to the institution of collective bargaining. A series of massive strikes of truck drivers led by Trotskyites in Minneapolis brought on class warfare and forced the recognition of the union. A similar upheaval that started on the docks in San Francisco was the prelude to both a general strike in the Bay Area and to a coastwide maritime shutdown. The result was recognition of the longshore union, led by radical Harry Bridges, and the establishment of collective bargaining. The largest of these strikes took place during the fall of 1934 when 376,000 textile workers in hundreds of mills in New England and the South walked out.

The great strikes of 1934 confirmed Senator Wagner in his conviction that the nation needed a new labor policy. The National Labor Relations Board, which worked out a "common law" of policy in its cases, but confronted the same problem of noncompliance by die-hard employers that had destroyed NLB, agreed. Wagner's staff and the NLRB revised the bill and on February 21, 1935, the senator introduced the proposed National Labor Relations Act. Again, there was a sharp conflict over the measure between labor and management; but this time Roosevelt, who did not support it strongly, did not intervene to put it aside. Congress passed the bill with large majorities, and on July 5, the President signed the Wagner Act.

The theory of the statute was that there was an "inequality of bargaining power between employees who do not possess full freedom of association . . . and employers who are organized in the corporate or other forms of ownership association. . . ." Congress sought to redress this imbalance by protecting the right of workers to organize and by encouraging collective bargaining. The new, permanent, three-member National Labor Relations Board would achieve these objectives in two ways. The first was by designating employee representatives for the purpose of collective bargaining. Here the Board would determine the appropriate unit, that is, the specific employees who would be eligible to vote in a representation election and the precise jobs in the plant that would later be covered by a collective bargaining agreement. It would then conduct a secret-ballot election, and, if a majority within the unit voted for a union, the Board would certify that it was "the exclusive representative of all the employees" in the unit.

The other function of the Board was to prevent employers from engaging in five designated "unfair labor practices." The first, following the language of Section 7(a), was to restrain employees from self-organization and concerted activities in forming, joining, or assisting labor unions for the purpose of collective bargaining. The second prohibition on employer activity was to dominate a labor organization, in effect, outlawing the company union. The third was to discriminate among employees by such practices as hiring, firing, and paying special wage rates in order to encourage or discourage membership in a labor organization. The main purpose was to bar the employer from discharging a worker who had joined the union. The fourth was to prohibit an employer from firing a worker who filed charges with or testified before the NLRB. Finally, it became an unfair practice for an employer "to refuse to bargain collectively" with the certified representative elected by a majority of employees. There were no unfair practices for labor unions.

The Wagner Act afforded an unprecedented opportunity to the American labor movement. Corporations hostile to unions were determined that the law should not be enforced. Their basic strategy was to challenge the constitutionality of the statute. A group of lawyers under the auspices of the American Liberty League opined that the Wagner Act was invalid, thereby encouraging noncompliance. Employers tied up the NLRB with injunction suits for almost two years. On April 12, 1937, however, the Supreme Court upheld the constitutionality of the statute by a five to four vote in five related cases, the most notable involving the Jones & Laughlin Steel Corporation.

Ironically, at this moment of victory, the labor movement split on the issue of craft vs. industrial unionism. That question had been papered over with an ambiguous compromise at the AFL's San Francisco convention in 1934. By the next year the pressure for the chartering of new industrial unions in the mass production industries had increased significantly but was frustrated on every side by craft control of the Federation and its Executive Council, particularly by unions in the building and metal trades.

At the Federation's Atlantic City convention in October, 1935, John L. Lewis and his followers, recognizing they were in the minority, decided to force the industrial union issue. After bitter debate over a resolution to charter new industrial unions, which the craft unionists defeated, the Lewis group got thirty-eight percent of the vote, more than expected. Near the close of the convention, "Big Bill" Hutcheson, president of the Carpenters and the most powerful of the craft unionists, interrupted a speech by a Rubber Workers delegate to demand a point of order. Lewis called this "small potatoes." Hutcheson called Lewis "a bastard." The miner caught the carpenter on the jaw with a swift jab and sent him sprawling. Lewis adjusted his necktie, relit his cigar, and sauntered off. Hutcheson won the point of order, but Lewis and industrial unionism got the headlines.

At a breakfast meeting the day after the convention Lewis called together a group of industrial unionists to lay the groundwork for a new organization, the Committee for Industrial Organization (CIO). Lewis became chairman. Charles P. Howard was named secretary. President of one of the purest craft organizations in the Federation, the Typographical Union, Howard believed industrial unionism was the only way to organize the mass industries. John Brophy, a miner, became director.

While CIO would launch organizing drives, it stressed at the outset that they would be in "affiliation" with the AFL, thus avoiding dual unionism. But Lewis and Green soon denounced each other publicly, and fratricide became the condition of the labor movement. In August, 1936, the Executive Council suspended the ten affiliated unions that composed the CIO. In November the Tampa convention, with the industrial unionists absent, expelled them from the Federation. In 1938 the CIO proclaimed itself a dual trade union federation and changed its name to the *Congress* of Industrial Organizations.

Both the CIO and the AFL moved vigorously into organizing the unorganized, but the former made the dramatic gains. For Lewis, steel was the prime target. His first task was to capture the old Amalgamated Association of Iron, Steel and Tin Workers, not for its strength but for its industrial union charter. Granted many years before by the AFL, the charter would lend legitimacy to the drive. This was accomplished on June 4, 1936, when the Amalgamated joined CIO and merged into the newly formed Steel Workers Organizing Committee whose chairman was Philip Murray, vice-president of the Miners.

Murray established headquarters in Pittsburgh and recruited an able staff. SWOC's strategy was threefold: work with the ethnic groups that composed the industry's labor force; exploit the federal government, particularly the Senate's La Follette Committee, which was exposing antiunion practices; and, most important, capture the restive company unions from within. This last was especially effective in the mills of United States Steel, the largest corporation in the industry. By the end of 1936 "Big Steel's" chairman Myron C. Taylor, concluding that Murray had won over the company unions, entered into secret negotiations with Lewis that led to the signing of a collective bargaining agreement on March 2, 1937.

In the wake of this sensational victory, SWOC swept up many smaller firms. By April it claimed a membership of 280,000. Murray now turned his attention to Jones & Laughlin, the fourth firm in the industry, which had challenged the constitutionality of the Wagner Act in the Supreme Court and lost. SWOC shut down J & L for two days in May. An NLRB election followed, which the union won handily, and an agreement was signed.

The other so-called "Little Steel" companies—Bethlehem, Republic, Youngstown, National, and Inland—proved much tougher. Their executives were bitterly antiunion. Led by Tom Girdler of Republic, and excepting only the officers of Inland, they were committed to the use of violence. When orders for steel fell off in May, 1937, a prelude to recession, they welcomed a walkout as a test of strength they expected to win. Late that month Girdler forced Murray into a strike for which SWOC was not yet ready. It gradually spread to most of the other companies which continued to operate, and there was much violence. In the "Memorial Day Massacre" at Republic's South Chicago mill, Chicago police killed ten people and wounded many others.

This defeat for SWOC was the turning point in the strike. By the end of June the union had gained only limited recognition at Inland and Youngstown mills in Indiana. This caused Lewis to become extremely annoyed with Roosevelt because the President refused to support SWOC in the Little Steel strike.

The United Automobile Workers (UAW) emerged as a major union at the same time, but under markedly different conditions. Several small auto unions that had popped up in the NRA period and made limited gains in calling strikes and negotiating contracts amalgamated into the UAW in April, 1936, under the presidency of Homer Martin, a former Baptist preacher. In July the union, firmly committed to industrial organization, affiliated with CIO. Its main task was to organize the Big Three of the industry—General Motors, Ford, and Chrysler. The UAW began with GM, by far the largest with 110 plants in fourteen states and eighteen foreign countries.

During the latter part of 1936 the UAW pushed organization throughout the GM system, especially in Flint, Michigan. At this time the sit-down strike emerged as an effective organizing weapon. There was a rash of sit-downs by new unions between 1936 and 1938, notably the Goodyear strike in Akron in 1936. The UAW adopted the technique enthusiastically and forced the largest manufacturing corporation in the world to stop production. What some consider the greatest strike of a turbulent decade was on.

The sit-down continued in Flint for six weeks. Michigan governor Frank Murphy called in the National Guard, not to evict the strikers but to keep the peace. He then moved to mediation, involving Lewis and GM's top officials along with Secretary of Labor Frances Perkins and the President. On February 11, 1937, Murphy got an agreement. The UAW evacuated the plants; in return the union gained recognition. The UAW was now established in GM.

This great victory was followed by agreements at Hudson, Packard, and Studebaker, along with many parts manufacturers. On April 6, Chrysler signed a contract with the union. The UAW now launched a drive to organize Ford. Henry Ford was utterly opposed to collective bargaining, and his Service Department, headed by Harry Bennett, was a violence squad.

Two UAW organizers, Walter Reuther and Richard Frankensteen, were beaten unmercifully at the "Battle of the Overpass" outside the River Rouge plant on May 26, 1937. The union deferred the Ford campaign.

A number of smaller CIO unions made notable gains. The National Maritime Union, with important communist influence, organized the sailors on the East and Gulf coasts after a series of violent strikes. In 1937 Harry Bridges took his West Coast longshoremen out of the AFL International Longshoremen's Association and formed the International Longshoremen's and Warehousemen's Union with a CIO charter. The United Rubber Workers, founded in 1935, effectively organized Firestone, Goodrich, U.S. Rubber, and Goodyear. The United Electrical, Radio and Machine Workers, also with a significant communist group of leaders, won agreements at General Electric, Westinghouse, RCA, and a host of smaller firms. GE, unusual for very large corporations, agreed to NLRB elections rather than risk strikes. Sidney Hillman's Amalgamated Clothing Workers formed a Textile Workers' Organizing Committee in 1937 which was only marginally successful in the widely dispersed industry.

The AFL responded vigorously to the CIO challenge. Ironically, craft unions which had fought Lewis over industrial unionism now organized on an industrial basis. While the Federation affiliates enjoyed no great conquests like U.S. Steel and GM, they gathered support in a very large number of smaller plants. The Teamsters, for example, had 441,000 members in 1939, substantially more than SWOC or the UAW and only slightly fewer than the UMW.

The result of the contest between AFL and CIO was

a dramatic increase in overall union membership. According to the Bureau of Labor Statistics, American unions (excluding Canadian members) hit the low point of 2,689,000 members in 1932. In 1935, the time of the AFL-CIO split, the total had grown to 3,584,000. By 1939 membership exceeded eight million.

Despite organized labor's gains, the specter of insecurity remained for the worker and his family. To compensate for loss of employment, other industrial nations had developed social insurance programs, but the United States had lagged behind. The only significant public program consisted of a group of uneven state workmen's compensation laws dealing with job-related illness and disease.

The Great Depression energized the impulse for social insurance. The two key movements were for unemployment insurance and old-age pensions. Wisconsin pioneered in enacting an unemployment insurance law in 1932. The need for pensions prompted the Townsend Plan, which emerged in 1933 and quickly won large public support. Under this nostrum, the government would pay everyone sixty years old or over $200 a month on the condition that the pension was spent within a month.

Roosevelt and Miss Perkins had long been committed to social insurance. In 1934 the President concluded that the time was ripe to develop a comprehensive federal program. He created the Committee on Economic Security with Miss Perkins as chairwoman. CES delivered the security bill to the White House in January, 1935, and the President immediately asked Congress to pass it. Both houses acted favorably after considerable revision, and on August 14, 1935, Roosevelt signed what had now come to be called the Social Security Act.

The statute contained a basket of programs, though there were several significant exclusions. The first of the new plans was a federal-state system of unemployment insurance. The role of the federal government was limited essentially to collecting and disbursing funds and to setting standards for the states, while the latter would determine most of the substantive features of the program. Many classes of employees were excluded from coverage—farm workers, domestic servants, public employees, employees of nonprofit organizations, among others. For firms with eight or more employees covered by social security, the government would impose a tax, starting at one percent of payroll in 1936 and rising to three percent in 1938. If the states enacted unemployment compensation laws, which all soon did, their employers would receive credit for ninety percent of the tax used to finance the state's program.

The Social Security Act established two programs for the aged, one for immediate needs, the other, a long-term pension system. The former, called old-age assistance, was a federal-state relief program in which the federal government would match a state contribution of no more than fifteen dollars a month. More important in the long run was the federal program of old-age social insurance. Under it, the worker would be taxed during his productive years thereby earning a pension for the time when he was no longer able to work. His employer would be taxed as a cost of production. The amount of the pension would be determined by the resources of the system. The law also created several welfare programs for especially needy groups beyond the aged. One was for families headed by women; the other was assistance to the blind.

There were two important exclusions from the Social Security Act. While most of the people who worked on the draft bill, including Roosevelt, favored the creation of a health insurance system, opposition of the American Medical Association made it politically impossible. The other exclusion was a general relief program. Although Hopkins urged a permanent welfare provision along with creation of a new department of welfare with Cabinet status, Roosevelt preferred to treat this problem separately on the theory that mass unemployment was temporary.

The emergency unemployment relief law was due to expire in 1935. Roosevelt and Hopkins agreed that it should be replaced with a new program that would stress work relief over direct relief. In 1935 the President established the Works Progress Administration for this purpose under Hopkins. By early 1936 over three million persons were at work in WPA programs, encompassing public buildings, schools, roads, parks, arts, theater, among others.

On taking office in 1933, Roosevelt and Miss Perkins were convinced of the need for federal standards legislation. The NRA codes provided for minimum wages and maximum hours, but the National Industrial Recovery Act was held unconstitutional in 1935. The cause seemed even more hopeless the next year when the Court voided the New York minimum wage law for women and children.

But in 1937 the judicial prospect brightened. The President proposed a reorganization of the Supreme Court which, while defeated, led to more liberal decisions, notably in the cases upholding the constitutionality of the Wagner Act. The Administration then proposed the Fair Labor Standards bill. It suffered a tortured legislative history with bitter opposition from the South, which sought to lure northern industry with low wages, long hours, and child labor. But in 1938, after significant concessions on standards and especially on coverage, Congress acted favorably and the President signed the Fair Labor Standards Act.

The statute established a minimum wage for a restricted number of covered industries in interstate commerce of twenty-five cents an hour in 1939, thirty cents in 1940, and forty cents in 1945. It also fixed the norm of the forty-hour week, again gradually. It became forty-four hours in 1939, forty-two hours in 1940, and forty hours thereafter. There was no prohibition on longer hours. Rather, the employer would have to pay at least time and a half for hours worked in excess of the weekly maximum. The law also prohibited the employment of children under sixteen years of age in most industries and under eighteen years in hazardous trades.

Unemployment remained high during the New Deal era. By 1935 a fifth of the labor force was still out of work. The only significant recovery occurred between 1935 and 1937. In the latter year, in fact, industrial production exceeded the level reached in 1929. But because of the growth of the labor force and increased productivity, there were still 7,700,000 persons unemployed. That number increased in the recession of

1937–38, exceeding ten million; 1939 yielded only a modest improvement. There were now almost nine and a half million persons out of work, over seventeen percent of the civilian labor force. While the New Deal policies broke the downward slide, they did not solve the current problem.

The outbreak of war in Europe in 1939 transformed the position of American labor. The mass unemployment of the thirties swiftly melted away as the nation turned to arming and supplying Britain and the Soviet Union along with building up its own military capability. By the time of Pearl Harbor there were shortages of skilled labor. The nation reached substantial full employment in 1942.

The rise in employment spurred a significant increase in union organization. It is probable that the labor movement added close to two million members between 1939 and 1941. By the latter year somewhere between one-fifth and one-fourth of nonagricultural employment was covered by union contract, the highest percentage in history to that time.

As before, black workers constituted the most disadvantaged group in the American labor force. A large number of unions, particularly craft organizations affiliated with the AFL, denied them membership. They were, in the words of the old saying, "the last to be hired and the first to be fired." When a black man was lucky enough to get a job, he often found himself behind a broom.

During the New Deal period millions of jobless black workers became important beneficiaries of the federal policy of nondiscrimination. Both FERA and

WPA provided relief without regard to race, creed, color, or national origin. But eligibility for relief did not meet the fundamental problem—a job. Rising employment in the defense period offered the prospect of dealing with this basic issue if historic discrimination could be overcome.

A. Philip Randolph, who was both an important black trade unionist as president of the Brotherhood of Sleeping Car Porters and a leading civil rights spokesman for the black community, saw the opportunity. In early 1941 jobs were opening up in defense plants, but they were not being offered to blacks. Randolph recognized that it would take government intervention to attack discrimination, and that Roosevelt would have to be forced to act by a dramatic gesture. He conceived of a Negro March on Washington.

The March was scheduled for July 1, 1941. In May the President became convinced that Randolph had strong backing and that the demonstration would be of great size. Through Eleanor Roosevelt and Mayor Fiorello H. LaGuardia of New York, the President sought to persuade Randolph to cancel the March. He refused. Invited to the White House, Randolph told Roosevelt that the price for calling off the demonstration was an executive order dealing with discrimination in defense plants.

On June 25, 1941, the President issued Executive Order No. 8802, which barred discrimination in employment in defense industries and created the Committee on Fair Employment Practices to investigate complaints and to correct valid grievances.

Nondiscrimination got another boost with the rise

of the CIO. The UMW had long accepted black miners on an equal footing with white. The new industrial unions, like SWOC and the UAW, adopted the same policy and black workers in these industries eagerly joined the unions.

Both SWOC and the UAW had left unfinished campaigns in 1937 that they now carried to substantial completion. The steel union filed unfair practice charges against the Little Steel companies, which NLRB and the courts upheld. Republic Steel was ordered to reinstate over 7,000 strikers with back pay. In early 1941 SWOC launched a massive organization campaign, selecting Bethlehem as the prime target. This led to NLRB elections in the big mills at Lackawanna, New York; Johnstown, Pennsylvania; and Sparrows Point, Maryland. All were won by large majorities. The victories broke the back of opposition at Republic, Youngstown Sheet & Tube, and Inland. By November, 1941, the NLRB had certified SWOC as bargaining agent for the employees of all four corporations.

The unfinished task of the UAW was to organize the Ford Motor Company. Following the stinging defeat he administered to the union in the Battle of the Overpass in 1937, Harry Bennett through his Service Department maintained an antiunion reign of terror in the factories. Henry Ford himself publicly denounced the UAW declaring: "Labor union organizations are the worst thing that ever struck the earth." The union, fettered by the recession and torn by internal factionalism, filed a series of unfair practice charges with the NLRB. The company, in an appeal to the courts, won one case in which Ford's statements were protected as freedom of speech under the First Amendment. The other cases were an uninterrupted series of UAW victories.

The union launched a major drive with CIO help in the fall of 1940. It gained a large membership and on April 2, 1941, the workers struck the River Rouge. Governor Murray D. Van Wagoner of Michigan mediated a settlement in which the strikers returned to work in return for Ford's consent to NLRB elections. The AFL made a belated entrance. In the voting on May 21, the UAW won overwhelmingly at the Rouge.

The election results—only 2.6 percent of the Rouge workers voted for no union—shocked Henry Ford. Further, the NLRB was about to open hearings that would expose Service Department violence and racketeering. Ford ordered Bennett to get a quick agreement with the UAW. The results were extraordinary. Wages became the highest in the industry. Layoffs and rehires would be based strictly on seniority. The Service Department was disbanded. The UAW won the union shop and the checkoff. Ford cars would carry the union label.

It was during this period that Franklin D. Roosevelt and John L. Lewis locked horns. In January, 1940, Lewis told Roosevelt that he would support him for a third term "if the vice-presidential candidate should happen to be John L. Lewis." Roosevelt thought the proposition ridiculous. That October, Lewis in a famous radio speech denounced the President and called upon labor to vote for Wendell Willkie, the Republican contender. If Roosevelt won, Lewis would consider the result "a vote of no-confidence" and would

resign as president of the CIO. Labor rejected Lewis
and voted overwhelmingly to reelect Roosevelt for a
third term.

At the CIO convention in November, Lewis tried
to go back on his promise, but Sidney Hillman skillfully forced him out. Phillip Murray became the president of the CIO. Lewis, wounded and bitter, went
home to the UMW.

The strike problem became a critical issue during
the defense period. There were a number of reasons—
rising employment, growing inflation, residual resistance by management to unionization, the inexperience
of new bargainers on both sides of the table, and the
exploitation of unrest by communist leaders within
the CIO unions they controlled. While the number of
work stoppages and workdays lost did not increase
significantly in 1940, several strikes directly affected
defense production. Antiunion spokesmen in industry
and Congress denounced the walkouts as "treason" and
demanded antistrike legislation.

In 1941 the situation worsened. A communist-led
UAW local shut down Allis-Chalmers in Milwaukee,
stopping the production of machinery essential for
naval vessels. Even more serious, communists called
out the UAW local at North American Aviation in
Inglewood, California. In all, the year saw more than
4,000 work stoppages, with 2,360,000 workers involved.

On March 19, 1941, the President by executive order
established the National Defense Mediation Board.
It was a tripartite agency with three public, four
industry, and four labor members (two each from the
AFL and the CIO). NDMB's function was to settle

labor disputes in defense industries. Its methods were mediation, voluntary arbitration, and, if they failed, fact-finding with recommendations which might be made public.

In the ten months of its life the Board received a total of 118 disputes. In most cases, strikes were in progress when the agency entered the dispute; in a number of others, stoppages soon took place. NDMB policy was to persuade the union to call off the strike in return for a promise of a hearing and of wage retroactivity to the date of expiration of the contract or of the time of return to work. This was successful in the majority of cases. If, however, one of the parties refused to accept the recommendation, the Board forwarded the matter to the White House.

NDMB's greatest case involved the captive mines. At stake was the output of the basic steel industry, essential to the entire defense program. Lewis had won the union shop in the commercial mines in 1939. Two years later he demanded the same provision from the twelve major steel corporations for their coal mines. Only Jones & Laughlin agreed. The UMW called out 50,000 miners at the others on September 15, 1941. Secretary of Labor Frances Perkins immediately certified the dispute to the Board. Lewis agreed to send the men back to work for thirty days while the NDMB engaged in fruitless mediation.

Roosevelt appealed to the miners' patriotism not to strike again, which enraged Lewis. He called a second strike on October 27. On the condition of submission of the union shop issue to the Board, he then agreed to send the men back into the pits on November 3, for fifteen days. On November 10, the Board by a vote of nine to two came out against the union shop, only CIO members Murray and Tom Kennedy of the UMW voting for it. These men resigned and NDMB collapsed. Roosevelt himself now entered the negotiations, but with equally dismal results.

Lewis called a third strike on November 17. The next day the President got both sides to agree to binding arbitration before a board consisting of Lewis, Benjamin Fairless of U.S. Steel, and Dr. John R. Steelman, the director of the U.S. Conciliation Service. Lewis, certain that Steelman would vote for the union shop, ordered the miners back to work. The award was as Lewis expected, but hardly anyone noticed. It came down on December 7, 1941, the day Japanese aircraft attacked Pearl Harbor.

President Roosevelt convened a labor-management conference at the White House on December 17. It consisted of the twelve top labor leaders (six from the AFL and six from the CIO) and an equal number of prominent employers. William H. Davis and Senator Elbert D. Thomas of Utah, chairman of the Senate Committee on Education and Labor, were the moderators. The conference reached unanimous agreement on two basic policies. The first prohibited strikes and lockouts for the duration of the war. The second provided that labor disputes would be submitted to a government board for resolution. Taken together, these principles insured compulsory arbitration and guaranteed uninterruped production. Conflict developed over union security. The employers insisted that the board should be denied jurisdiction over this issue; labor demanded the right to consider the question. Roosevelt cut the knot on December 23, announcing that he accepted the two endorsed principles. Asserting that the agency would have authority over "all disputes," he sustained the labor position on union security.

On January 12, 1942, the President issued an executive order creating the tripartite National War Labor Board of twelve members, four each from labor, industry, and the public. Davis became chairman; Professor George W. Taylor of the University of Pennsylvania, vice-chairman. Most of its dispute procedures were like those of the Defense Mediation Board, but it would also issue "directive orders," that is, final decisions. NWLB inherited the NDMB's unfinished cases. The NWLB's jurisdiction extended to disputes that "might interrupt work which contributes to the effective prosecution of the war." In the exigencies of wartime this became, in effect, virtually the entire economy. The agency's authority stemmed from the President's powers as commander-in-chief. Despite the urging of some, including Lewis, that it begin with a statement of principles, the Board chose to hammer out policies on a case-by-case basis.

In a series of decisions in the first half of 1942, NWLB evolved a standard maintenance-of-membership compromise. The employee was free to join or to decline membership in the union. If he enrolled, he was obligated to maintain his membership as a condition of employment for the life of the contract.

Far more important was the shaping of wartime wage policy, notably in the Little Steel decision of July 16, 1942. SWOC had won bargaining rights at

Bethlehem, Republic, Youngstown, and Inland before Pearl Harbor, but the parties had failed to negotiate their first contracts largely because of a disagreement over wages. The union asked for an increase of twelve and a half cents an hour, or a dollar a day, justified basically by the rise in the cost of living. The corporations argued that it was inflationary, particularly with a basic material like steel, where the higher cost would be passed along to many consuming industries.

In the Little Steel case the majority on the wage issue consisted of the NWLB's public and industry members, with the labor group in dissent. Taylor wrote the opinion, which became the core of wartime wage policy. His theory was the maintenance of pre-war real wages. This would both protect the worker's income against the erosion of rising prices and at the same time prevent him from exploiting the tight wartime labor market by increasing his real wages. Between January 1, 1941, when the inflation began, and May 1, 1942, living costs had risen fifteen percent. Since steelworkers had already gotten 11.8 percent in wage increases, they were now entitled to the added 3.2 percent. Taylor proposed an additional 2.3 percent because the case had been certified to the Board before the President's anti-inflation message and because the cost of living had advanced more in steel towns than the national average. Thus, Little Steel employees received a five and a half percent increase— forty-four cents a day. More important, the national standard, subject to certain adjustments, became a fifteen percent rise in hourly wage rates from the base date of January 1, 1941. The Little Steel decision was an incomplete wage stabilization policy because, under NWLB's authority, it applied only to dispute cases in that sector of the economy covered by collective bargaining. Many employers, both nonunion and union, were starting to grant substantial wage increases voluntarily in order to hold or pirate labor on the assumption that the government would bear the added cost. At the urging of the President, therefore, Congress passed the Economic Stabilization Act to maintain prices, wages, and salaries at their levels of September 15, 1942. On October 3, Roosevelt issued an executive order granting NWLB authority over virtually all wages and many salaries under $5,000; the Commissioner of Internal Revenue received control over higher salaries.

The Little Steel formula became the Board's basic wage policy. If a wage increase would cause a price increase, it could be put into effect only if approved by the Director of Economic Stabilization, former Supreme Court Justice James F. Byrnes. The result of this order was both to broaden the Board's jurisdiction and to circumscribe its powers. From that time forward, organized labor conducted a massive campaign to exploit, outflank, and shatter the wage stabilization program. Very low wages moved up to the Fair Labor Standards Act minimum. Women began to receive equal pay with men.

A very wide range of "inequalities" was discovered until the "hold-the-line" order of April 8, 1943, stripped the Board of authority to grant approval for this reason. Individual workers received merit increases and promotions; and many industrial workers won fringe benefits such as paid holidays, paid vacations, and shift differentials for the first time.

In the latter part of 1943 the AFL and CIO joined to attack the Bureau of Labor Statistics' Cost-of-Living Index, the yardstick under Little Steel. Labor claimed that BLS, because it failed to account for wartime price conditions, grossly understated the rise in living costs. Between January, 1941, and December, 1943, the index rose 23.4 percent. The AFL and CIO contended that costs had actually increased 43.5 percent. A technical committee under the chairmanship of economist Wesley C. Mitchell estimated that BLS had understated the price advance by from three to five percentage points. But this led to no change in Little Steel because the Board was powerless to alter the formula and neither the stabilization director nor the President would do so.

Several strong unions launched direct assaults upon the Little Steel policy. The nonoperating railway organizations, which had sought twenty cents, received eight cents from an emergency board and saw it cut to four cents under the formula by the stabilization director. They ordered a strike on December 30, 1943, and the operating unions joined in the call. Roosevelt directed the Army to take over the railroads.

Lewis presented the prime challenge to the wage stabilization program in the spring of 1943. Though the UMW's bituminous agreements had expired and the miners had exhausted their Little Steel entitlement, Lewis demanded an increase of two dollars a day and portal-to-portal pay—that is, compensation for nonproductive travel time from the mine entrance to the working face and return. Lewis refused to appear at a War Labor Board hearing, and the miners began to strike. The President seized the mines and named Interior Secretary Harold Ickes as administrator. NWLB then denied the wage increase and referred the portal-to-portal issue to the parties. When no agreement was reached on June 11, the miners resumed the strike, this time against the government. There was great public outrage against Lewis, and Congress moved to pass the punitive Smith-Connally War Labor Disputes bill, which restricted the right to strike. On June 18, the Board ordered him to sign the contract. Lewis called it a "yellow-dog" and refused. On June 23, Roosevelt said he would ask Congress for authority to draft striking miners into the Army.

In late October the miners again walked out, and the President again seized the mines. Ickes then worked out a settlement with Lewis, and the men returned to work on November 3, 1943. In fact, the miners won an increase of a dollar and a half a day. But it was taken as fringe benefits in a combination of portal-to-portal pay and a shorter lunch period rather than as a direct wage increase. Thus, NWLB could approve the settlement technically under the Little Steel formula.

Until the latter part of 1942, manpower needs were met by tapping the depression reservoir of the unemployed. From that time forward there was a shortage of labor which became progressively more severe.

These labor needs were met in two ways—by raising the number of persons in the labor force (mainly by hiring women, teen-agers, and retirees) and by increasing the hours of work. War plants shifted from a forty-hour to a forty-eight-hour workweek; in 1943, labor shortage areas also adopted the forty-eight-hour week. Under the Fair Labor Standards Act the workers received time and a half pay for hours over forty. This made the enforcement of the War Labor Board's Little Steel policy workable. That is, weekly earnings might rise significantly despite the restraint the formula imposed on hourly rates.

In April, 1942, the President established the War Manpower Commission under Paul V. McNutt, the former governor of Indiana, to allocate available labor in the face of the wartime shortage. In the spring of 1943 McNutt issued a sweeping order intended to "freeze" about twenty-seven million essential workers in their jobs, which angered the AFL and the CIO. The military and many others urged national service legislation, or a "labor draft." The labor movement violently opposed the idea. Roosevelt concurred until January, 1944, when, worn out by the 1943 coal strikes, he endorsed national service as part of a package that would also have imposed heavy burdens on industry. The House adopted a labor draft bill in 1945, but the collapse of Germany made the issue moot.

The wartime labor shortage significantly improved the economic status of two groups which had suffered historic discrimination— women and blacks. The number of females employed soared as "men's" jobs, particularly in the blue-collar categories, opened up; the War Labor Board's policy of equal pay for equal work eliminated wage differentials based on sex. Blacks also made progress, though overcoming discrimination proved difficult. There was a vicious race riot in Detroit in 1943. The FEPC, despite this formidable opposition, succeeded in opening a large number of jobs in war industries and government to black workers.

The sharp increase in employment during the war caused a dramatic growth in union membership. By 1945 more than fourteen million American workers were enrolled. Equally significant, the union proportion of nonagricultural employment reached an all-time high of 35.8 percent. By the end of the war the trade-union movement was big and had established firm collective bargaining bases in most of the important industries of the United States.

*In the single generation after World War II, women's share
of jobs rose from about a quarter to nearly a half.
Alyce Jackson,* American Education Magazine.

★ 6 ★

UNIONS AND RIGHTS
IN THE SPACE AGE

by Jack Barbash

World War II forced the integration of the newer
unions into the war effort and forced business into
working out accommodations with the unions for the
duration. Absent the urgency of war, business might
not have conceded industrial union power quite so
quickly. In this sense, World War II and its immediate aftermath represent a period of consolidation of
union power. This was followed successively by containment, which began with the enactment of the
Taft-Hartley law, and renewal, as evidenced by the
eruption of public-sector unionism in the early 1960s.

Wartime controls inevitably built up tensions within
the rank and file. With the war's end, a wave of nationwide strikes battered the maritime, railroad, coal, oil,
auto, electrical, telephone, and steel industries; four
and a half million workers were on the picket lines
during the strike wave in 1946. The strike wave had
its economic source in the massive reconversion from
war to peace as the unions sought to make up "the cut
in take-home pay" caused by reduced overtime, unemployment, downgrading, price rises, and increased
productivity. The unions argued heatedly that busi-

ness had been favored by liberal tax laws and generous terms for the renegotiation of contracts and disposal of surplus property. But no comparable solicitude had been shown for the "human side" of reconversion.

The strike wave moved bargaining into new salients. In the oil strike the government encouraged settlement through a fact-finding board. In the General Motors strike, the UAW at GM, under the leadership of Walter P. Reuther, marshaled a mass of data to support its claim that the union's demand for a thirty percent wage increase could be met without raising prices—an issue which was never really joined. In U.S. Steel, the wage-price relationship took a different twist. In effect, the company made its response to the union's wage demands contingent in the size of the product price increase, which the govrnment was prepared to grant. In meatpacking, the federal government seized the struck plants, which the CIO's Packinghouse Workers denounced as an act of strike-breaking. President Harry Truman resorted to seizure of the railroads and threatened strikers with military conscription. But at the last minute the unions pulled back and called off the strike. In Western Electric the National Federation of Telephone Workers, a reconverted company union, proved its independence by engaging in a series of militant strikes. A New York strike of 30,000 longshoremen dramatized the inter- and intra-union conflict on the waterfront.

The strike wave gave additional momentum to restrictive legislation. The Lea Act prohibiting musician featherbedding in radio stations and the Hobbs Anti-Racketeering Act were passed in 1946. A year later the

Wagner Act was amended by the Taft-Hartley Act. Authored by Senator Robert Taft of Ohio and Representative Fred Hartley of New Jersey, the Act reflected the ebbing of union political influence and the corresponding rise of business influence in the first Republican Congress since 1930. The underlying philosophy of Taft-Hartley was to balance off the Wagner Act restrictions on employers with restrictions against unions. Denounced by unions as a "slave-labor act," the Taft-Hartley Act outlawed the closed shop, jurisdictional strikes, and secondary boycotts. Union power in emergency disputes, political contributions, and negotiated health and welfare funds were curtailed. Union officials were required to file non-communist affidavits. States were allowed to enact "right-to-work" laws, which created the so-called 14(b) issue. The injunction was reinstated to restrain boycotts, jurisdictional strikes, and national emergency walkouts. The National Labor Relations Board was bifurcated into separate prosecuting and judicial arms. Taft-Hartley established a new legal equilibrium in the union-management relationship less favorable to unions.

Taft-Hartley was brought about by both long- and short-run causes. From its passage on, the Wagner Act had been subjected to a continuous pressure for amendment by business and by AFL craft unions for whom the NLRB administration of the act was biased in favor of the industrial unions. Moreover, unionism had become "big unionism," and with it, as public-opinion polls showed, pro-union sentiment declined. The legislative history of the law makes plain the specific big-union targets: John L. Lewis, James C. Petrillo, the building trades unions, communist unionism, and large-scale strikes of the 1945–46 variety. Each represented an archetype for a particular Taft-Hartley provision.

On balance, Taft-Hartley and right-to-work legislation may have hurt the weak unions more than the strong. The Textile Workers found the more liberal free speech granted to employers the strongest obstacle to their southern organizing efforts. For the settled unions Taft-Hartley, aside from its reenforcement of containment influences, does not seem to have been an independent influence of determinable consequences. It is possible to speculate that the law forced a psychological withdrawal of labor leaders and created a more narrow focus. The unions against which Taft-Hartley provisions were specifically aimed—the miners, building trades, musicians—seem not to have been seriously hurt by the law. The "slave-labor law" epithet hurled at Taft-Hartley was clearly a case of propaganda over-kill. For a decade or so Taft-Hartley and the right-to-work laws became a prime political issue for the unions and probably did more to bring unions energetically into federal and state politics than anything else.

Containment of union influence impelled the trade-union movement to reexamine the division within its ranks between AFL and CIO. It took twenty years for them finally to heal the breach and unite in a new, merged federation. Not until 1953 did unity negotiations begin to take hold. The AFL had earlier insisted that the CIO give up its identity and surrender its members to the AFL unions with the relevant jurisdiction; and later, that any unity move be premised on a "return to the house of labor"—the AFL. The CIO leadership found these terms unacceptable; over the years the affiliated unions had built a strong sense of identification with CIO.

For its part, the older AFL leadership regarded the CIO as upstarts mostly concerned with politicalizing the labor movement. The CIO people were just not their kind of trade unionists. The dominant sentiment in the CIO saw AFL leadership as unduly preoccupied with protecting vested jurisdictional interests. Philip Murray, speaking for CIO, resisted what AFL president William Green called "organic unity" and countered with a concept of "functional unity," which meant that the AFL and CIO would work together on matters of common concern but not necessarily enter into constitutional merger.

Final merger was preceded by two trial collaborations. First was the joint participation of the AFL and CIO in the founding of International Confederation of Free Trade Unions (ICFTU) in 1949. This represented an implicit concession of equality by the AFL to the CIO in the international labor movement and CIO recognition that international communism had a dark side for trade unionism. The second collaboration came in December, 1950, with the formation of the United Labor Policy Committee. ULPC was made up of AFL, CIO, the Railway Labor Executive Association, and the Machinists—who were then unaffiliated. "Our purpose," ULPC. announced, "is to develop a common approach to the problems arising out of the mobilization and stabilization program" deriving out of American involvement in the Korean action. Here, in effect, was Murray's functional unity, although the ULPC idea seems not to have been of CIO origin.

The deaths of William Green and Philip Murray

192 ★ A History of the American Worker

brought sudden changes in the top leadership of the AFL and CIO. Walter Reuther became CIO president, and George Meany acceded to the presidency of the AFL. Prospects for full merger suddenly revived in December of 1952. Meany announced that unity negotiations should start from a new beginning, which meant abandonment of "come back to the house of labor" as a precondition. For the first time in the unity negotiations, the AFL was offering the CIO partnership, not absorption.

The contrast between Meany and Green could not have been more marked. For Green the federation was mainly a barometer of national union interests; for Meany the federation was something more than the sum of its parts: It had a responsibility to initiate and to lead. Meany's exercise of federation leadership, allowing for differences in personal idiosyncrasies, has been in the CIO style of Lewis and Murray. Gompers was a leader, but he led by counsel and only rarely by sheer strength of will as has Meany. The labor movement became a national power center in Meany's time as it had never been under Gompers and Green.

At the first AFL-CIO unity meeting Meany proposed that the first step in unity negotiations be the consummation of a no-raid agreement. With minor changes, the AFL accepted the CIO draft. On December 5, 1955, the two labor organizations merged.

There are several reasons why the merger came when it did. The most important historical reason was that both AFL and CIO regarded the Eisenhower administration as essentially antagonistic to the interests of organized labor. While in the 1930s and 1940s both

AFL and CIO unions could grow concurrently, in the 1950s one union's expansion was perceived as coming at the expense of another. Separation had, therefore, become an indulgence in animosities which had lost their meaning.

A secondary reason—which by itself would not have been enough to have brought the CIO and AFL together—was that the passage of time had settled the spheres of influence of the affiliated unions and blunted much of the force of the craft vs. industrial union issue. The sphere-of-influence problems separating the AFL and CIO unions were found to be no more serious than those separating individual AFL unions from each other. Developments within the AFL and CIO made unified action easier. The CIO purged the communist-dominated unions from its ranks. The AFL expelled the racket-ridden longshoremen.

George Meany quickly applied his brand of leadership to the unity issue. He was the decisive influence in the federation's racket-union expulsions, and his resolute stand against readmission of the Teamsters had been enough to keep them out. The internal disputes agreement was also a major Meany achievement. The public policy stands of the federation have never been broader than in the Meany era. His forth-right position on civil rights—even as against affiliates—was spelled out before a House subcommitte in 1962:

". . . Corruption—like communism—seizes the leadership of a union and works down to lower levels by perverting the union's democratic procedures. The rank-and-file members are not consciously affected in their daily lives. They don't know what's going on, and they tend to dismiss published charges against the leadership as just another attack by a normally hostile press. Expulsion was the only way to convince the membership of this domination by corrupt elements. In most cases the members have rallied to new, clean unions or have overthrown the old leadership. But there is a big difference between corruption and discrimination. Discrimination is resisted at the top but perpetuated below. Discrimination represents the wrong-headedness of rank-and-file members; it is often maintained by unimpeachably democratic processes. Would we be better off to cast out these misguided members and remove them from the influence of the mainstream of the labor movement, meanwhile expelling in the same action the national leaders who deplore and fight discriminations? I think not. I think we can do more toward educating them if they're in the federation, with their own leaders getting broad AFL-CIO support toward the same end."

Under Meany the federation has manifested increased sensitivity to civil rights issues. At the federation's 1959 convention, Meany asked A. Philip Randolph, "Who in hell nominated you the guardian of all the Negroes in America?" At the 1963 convention, Meany referred to the black labor leader as "our own Phil Randolph." From the NAACP came the accolade: "The AFL-CIO has been one of the bulwarks of the Leadership Conference on Civil Rights which has been responsible for so much of the national legislation under which we now make progress."

The AFL-CIO's legislative representatives under Meany "work on a broader range of issues than any group in Washington." The first AFL-CIO priority of

1975 was a tax cut of more than twenty billion dollars keyed to lower- and middle-income taxpayers. Notable was the relative lack of emphasis on pure labor issues. The Federation's hard and unremitting anticommunist position in international policy—from which it has not been diverted by the easing of cold-war tensions in the post-Stalin years—also derived its main direction from Meany, as did the decision to remain neutral in the 1972 presidential elections.

The source of George Meany's power was not the national union from which he came—the Plumbers is a part, even though it has been helpful in winning acceptance for decisions otherwise distasteful to the building trades. This power is in large part the product of the great personal force exerted by a man who knows what he wants.

Meany's counterpart in the AFL-CIO merger, Walter Reuther, set forces in motion conducive to unity. First, he was committed to a unified labor movement as a matter of principle. Second, there was the threat from the United Steelworkers that if the CIO did not merge as a unit, individual unions would disaffiliate and join the AFL individually.

The union leader can hardly ever transcend the constraints of the economy, public policy, the employer's condition, inter- and intra-union power relationships, and the characteristic incrementalism of union strategy. The zone within which leadership charisma and "bossism" has to maneuver, therefore, is relatively narrow and, despite the dramatics which make it seem otherwise, the margin left for "pure" leadership is almost always very thin.

This is not to say that union leadership is "an ab-

stract force in the grip of an abstract mass," as Selig
Perlman once put it. On the contrary, what *matters* is
how well the union leader adjusts to his environment,
and this injects a large component of skill and craft in
the union leader's performance. The craft of union
leadership may frequently be more important to the
permanent life of the union than the quickly dissi-
pating asset of charisma. Reuther and Meany, in
different contexts, typify union leaders who represent
a large element of pure leadership, although they are
nonetheless products of their special situations. Reuther's leadership needed the scope allowed by a
dynamic growth industry. Meany needed a labor
movement with numbers and influence.

Walter Reuther, as the representative figure of
modern American industrial unionism, was a synthesis
of traditional business and socialist unionism. He was
the collective bargaining pace-setter of the postwar
period. It is no diminution of John L. Lewis's stature
to say that *his* major impact came in the industrial
union breakthrough at the start of this period but
was found wanting thereafter. Reuther, by contrast,
put his imprint on virtually every landmark in collective bargaining and trade unionism throughout this
period. The UAW's health care and pension policies
transformed the structure of employee compensation.
To be sure, Lewis had gotten it first, but in Reuther's
hands it became a program and a policy—characteristic words in his vocabulary—not a gamble. Reuther
dramatized the relevance of technological change—
"automation"—to collective bargaining as did no other
union leader. No other union, either, faced up more
squarely to the issue of communist penetration.

In the internal affairs of trade unionism the UAW under Reuther gave new content and meaning to workers' education, union democracy, skilled-worker representation, and civil rights at the workplace. He was the first union leader to raise the question of compatibility between collective bargaining and consumer prices: "We are not going to operate as a narrow economic pressure group which says, 'We are going to get ours and the public be damned.'" Whatever the temperamental qualities which may have been served thereby, strategically, Reuther's public relations acted to advance both rank-and-file and public understanding of the union's programs.

The new labor federation represented both historic continuities and contrasts. The most striking contrast with the past was the constitutional power conferred on the federation to deal with corruption, discrimination, and jurisdictional conflict in national union affiliates. Intervention by previous federation presidents had not been uncommon, but intervention was based on prestige of office and not on constitutional authority. Also noteworthy was labor leadership's acceptance of impartial outsiders functioning as quasi-judges in jurisdictional disputes—a field once regarded as the labor movement's own business.

Classical Gompers voluntarism—the labor movement's version of laissez-faire—was almost completely abandoned. Public policy began to occupy a central place on the unions' agenda. Only in respect to political nonpartisanship has the federation adhered to traditional ideology in the sense that it is formally neutral with respect to Democrats and Republicans. Much of this neutrality, however, is more formal than real because the labor movement has been, in a sense, a kind of union party within the national Democratic Party and many state Democratic parties, although a few enclaves of union influence exist in Republican state and local parties. The present union nonpartisanship is supported by a going political concern managed by union leaders who "belong" in the circles of political power. Nothing like this existed under the pre-1933 nonpartisanship, and it has constituted a difference in degree which has become a difference in kind.

The abandonment of voluntarism reflected the change in the underlying situation. Before voluntarism had become an unyielding dogma, the distrust of government intervention in economic affairs was derived from actual experience with government as a class state. Thus, for the Gompers era the state represented the *ex-parte* injunction, the "yellow dog" contract, and the use of the military as strikebreakers. It was John L. Lewis's special genius that he recognized and acted on the possibility that the state could also be responsive to the workers' mass political movement. The state could mean Wagner acts, social security, wage-hour laws, and full employment, as well as coercive power directed against unions.

Containment of unions by legal intervention advanced further with the enactment in 1959 of the Landrum-Griffin law. Where Taft-Hartley had addressed itself largely to containing union power in collective bargaining, Landrum-Griffin focused major attention on the relationship between union leaders and members. Landrum-Griffin's approach to containment consisted of (1) a "bill of rights" for union members,

(2) disclosure requirements for unions and union officers in respect to finances and possible "conflict of interest" transactions, (3) protections against improper trusteeships, and (4) safeguards against manipulation of union elections to favor incumbents.

The main target of the Landrum-Griffin law was the Teamsters and its then president, James R. Hoffa. The groundwork had been laid in an extensive investigation by a U.S. Senate committee chaired by Senator John McClellan of Arkansas, with Robert F. Kennedy as chief counsel. The investigation established a pattern for several unions of personal aggrandizement and enrichment through racketeering, penetration of racket control, use of union funds for personal business, and conflict-of-interest transactions between employers and employer "middlemen." In union internal affairs the investigators found abuses in democratic processes including coercion and intimidation of dissenting members, election frauds, and gross violations of members' civil rights.

The experience of Landrum-Griffin in the decade and a half of its operations suggests that the prohibited practices were marginal occurrences, but needed to be dealt with through public authority. No endemic problem of financial and democratic wrongdoing is apparent in American unions, if litigation under Landrum-Griffin is any guide. The law's most significant impact has been to make the position of challengers to incumbent officers more tenable. The relatively large turnover of union officers at all levels is mainly due to a wave of membership discontent stemming from the economic uncertainties of the times, but the availability of Landrum-Griffin remedies has made it more likely that the discontent can be asserted through union political processes without unduly favoring incumbents. Serious questions have been raised as to whether racket penetration has been effectively eliminated. The mysterious disappearance of Hoffa in 1975 is a dramatic indication that it has not.

In the late 1950s many union leaders became convinced that containment did not derive solely from government intervention; it was also functioning as a calculated management strategy. "Hard line," "hardening of attitudes," "hard bargaining," "stiffening of attitude by employers" variously expressed the temper of this strategy. A. H. Raskin of the *New York Times* saw a threat of "class warfare—low voltage, nonviolent but nonetheless destructive in its implications for industrial democracy." According to the hard-line model, automation was a management bargaining tactic, as were the management demands for major work rule changes notable in steel and railroads, contracting-out, tougher production standards, and plant relocations away from the centers of union concentration. The object of management's tougher bargaining stance was to recapture some of the rights surrendered, as business perceived it, during the "soft" bargaining of World War II and after.

Even as the unions were getting it from all sides, they were also remaking the worker's relation to his job and his employer. Landmark events included:

1950: UAW and GM negotiate five-year contract with pension, escalator clauses, annual improvement factor, and union shop.

Late 1950s: UAW and International Harvester experiment with methods of "deformalizing" grievance and arbitration procedures.

1954–55: UAW, USW, IUE, and URW advance guaranteed annual wage proposals which evolve into supplementary unemployment compensation plans.

1956: UMW opens ten new hospitals in Appalachia financed by the UMWA Retirement and Welfare Fund.

1959: Armour and Packinghouse Workers and Amalgamated Meat Cutters negotiate automation fund.

1959: USW and Kaiser Corporation establish Long Range Committee charged with considering "a long range plan for the equitable sharing of the company's progress between the stockholders, the employees and the public."

1960: Pacific Maritime Association and the West Coast longshore union under Harry Bridges conclude an historic "productivity bargaining" compact in which the quid pro quos are job security and relaxation of restrictive working rules.

1960: USW and basic steel industry establish Human Relations Research Committee.

1961: UAW and American Motors establish a profit-sharing, "progress-sharing" fund including an annual improvement factor and joint conference.

These experiments, in view of the complex nature of the problems being probed, did not always work out. Nevertheless, they did give witness to the vitality of collective bargaining as a vehicle both for channeling conflict and solving problems.

Another major watershed during this period was the gradual but material progress in building a comprehensive scheme of private social security through collective bargaining out of the piecemeal "fringe benefits" beginnings of the War Labor Board days. The program consisted of two major components: (1) offsets against wage losses due to illness, death, old age, and unemployment, and (2) insurance against the costs associated with illness; or to put it differently, health insurance, sick pay, pensions, supplemental unemployment benefits, and life insurance.

At first the trade unions sought to secure these benefits by the Wagner-Murray-Dingell bill in 1945-46; failing, the unions turned to stepwise improvement through collective bargaining—specifically: (1) preservation of the real value of existing benefits against erosion by rising costs; (2) deepening the protection afford by existing benefits—example: increasing hospitalization days; (3) spinning off new benefits, i.e., severance pay from SUB, diagnosis, medical care, dental care, etc., from the original hospitalization and surgical care; (4) shifting financing of benefits from employee to employer; (5) development of new institutions, skills, and professions to negotiate, evaluate, and administer the benefits.

Despite the automation debate—perhaps because of it—collective bargaining has, on the whole, worked well in accommodating to technological change. The methods of accommodation have included negotiation, attrition, gain sharing, transition procedures, and "buy-out"—or productivity bargaining. Collective bargaining appears to have established the general principle that employees have an equitable interest in their existing job conditions, and in the event of material impairment of this interest by technological change, merger, or relocation, the employee has a legitimate claim on his employer to offset in whole or in part the losses suffered as a consequence. Union-management confrontations over technology were most serious during this period in newspaper printing, railroading, and East Coast longshoring.

Grievance arbitration, also from War Labor Board momentum, became firmly established as a prime feature of the collective bargaining process. Although a working consensus among the participants has evolved, the unions have not hesitated to voice strenuous criticisms of the excessive cost, legalism, and delay which characterize the grievance-arbitration process. Managements have been critical of the arbitrator's "usurpation" of authority and the union's tendency to use grievance handling for its internal political purposes. There is recognition, however, of the common stake in the effectiveness of the process.

Containment there may have been in the dimensions of union membership and labor force penetration, but in collective bargaining, internal union affairs, and influence in politics and public policy the trade unions managed to stake out new and higher ground.

Renewal as the theme of union development from the mid-1960s on has meant that trade union membership recovered momentum mainly through a large infusion of public and quasi-public employee membership in the '60s and '70s. Tendencies which emerged in the period of containment continued over into renewal. The rank and file pressed their claims for self-determination more insistently and militantly. Check and balance from below became not only a constitutional fact but a working reality which a union leader ignored at his peril. Also in this period the state intervened in labor relations from a standpoint of positive public policy.

Renewal as the dominant theme of union development from the mid-1960s on has reflected the increase in union membership in each year but one since 1964. Even so, union membership has not kept pace with growth in the labor force and nonagricultural employment. The recruitment of white-collar workers (outside of government) into union membership produced meager results. Women account for a constantly rising percentage of union membership. But the dynamic element in union membership in this period was the government sector, which since 1956 has consistently gained both in number and percentage.

The upsurge of public unionism in the postindustrial era reflected the enormous expansion of employment in state and local government. Moreover, the momentum was initially generated by laws and executive orders which protected and encouraged unionization and collective bargaining. These encouraging laws must have tapped deep reservoirs of sentiment to have evoked such volatile responses. The public sector spark was first lighted by Mayor Wagner's recognition of public employees bargaining in New York City in 1959 and President Kennedy's promulgation of Executive Order 10988 in early 1962. This set off a tide of other legislation. Some states enacted their laws under the forced draft of employee militancy.

Another large influence on the eruption of public employee unionism was the almost decade-long uninterrupted period of economic expansion which gave governments the revenues with which to meet union demands for increased salaries and permitted the unions to demonstrate the efficacy of collective bargaining to their constituents. The high-level employment of the period also encouraged public employees to take risks in unionizing because other jobs were likely to be available if they lost.

The public sector eruption has been notable for the militancy of its "brinkmanship" strikes, of doctors, nurses, hospital workers, police, firefighters, sanitation workers, teachers, welfare workers; and among federal employees, air traffic controllers and postal employees. In the 1974-75 period of recession and inflation, the major strike issue was the deterioration of real wages and the severity of retrenchment layoffs in the cities.

Public sector unionism has been guided for the most part by union leaders with temperaments to match this spirit of the times. Albert Shanker moved up the ranks of teacher unionism and the larger labor movement. He has contended with all of the forces acting on urban education: from one direction the militant demands of teacher unions for job security and a kind of "codetermination" in educational policy; from the other the insistent pressures for community control, economy and efficiency, and preferential treatment in the recruitment and advancement of minority teachers. The media have pictured Shanker as a power machine, and almost no piece about him is complete without reference to his observation that "power is a good thing; it's better than powerlessness." But Shanker is more than a power machine. The point is that his style seems, from the teachers' viewpoint, to have paid off and galvanized all other teacher militancy.

The American Federation of State, County and Municipal Employees has produced notable militants in public sector unionism: Jerry Wurf, the union's president, succeeded Arnold Zander, its founder. The union under Zander was a prototype of the civil service union. Collective bargaining and striking were not rejected, but they were not primary either. Instead, in common with other government unions, AFSCME relied mainly on lobbying—"collective begging," as it was derisively called—for civil service legislation, the merit system, and legislative salary increases. Zander also put much effort on the formation of the Public Service International and the establishment of housing projects for union members.

Wurf reorganized AFSCME activity toward more direct collective bargaining, more militant unionism, and a more activist political style. He has "taken giant steps to change the tone and nature of this organization and to make it a real trade union with marrow in its bones and blood in its arteries." Strikes have become an essential part of that militancy and "the right to strike," excluding only police and firefighters, is something that Wurf, as he says "fights bitterly for."

Under Wurf the national union headquarters has taken on the new dynamism with which he has sought to permeate the organization. Organizing, bargaining, political and legislative action, education, staff training, civil rights have all become staff specializations infused with Wurf's hard-driving temperament. If there is such a thing as an "opposition" on the AFL-CIO

Executive Council, Wurf is it. He has made well known his discontents with the political orientation of AFL-CIO and with the fragmentation of jurisdiction in the public sector. Legislative alliances with the National Education Association are part of that opposition role.

Many of the public sector unions in state and local government are for the first time also unionizing low-wage workers—black, Mexican-American, and Puerto Rican. The Laborers and Service Employees, have also emerged as major growth unions with an organizing-centered leadership organizing workers who used to be considered "unorganizable."

Outside of the public sector the major upheaval has been among migrant agricultural workers. Under the leadership of Cesar Chavez, the economic and social structure of mass production agriculture in California is being remade. In the "factories in the field" of California, he built unionism by imbuing Chicano workers with racial pride and by making the union into a way of life for his people. He marshaled massive outside aid from the larger labor movement, most notably the AFL-CIO and the UAW, and also from the Catholic church. From committed young people he organized a kind of Peace Corps. The maintenance of the union and its auxiliary cooperatives and the powerful consumer boycott would not have been possible without this outside aid.

Chavez's ascetic life-style has had much to do with elevating farm unionism into an epic struggle. His *La Causa* appears more as a revolutionary and racial upheaval than a bargaining union, but is the weak side of his strength as far as trade unionism is concerned.

Chavez has also had to take on the more formidable Teamsters who, if a union has to be in the fields, is preferred by the growers. More than unionism is needed, in Chavez's philosophy: What is required is "a *movement* . . . an *idea*" by which the Chicano workers can achieve salvation on their *own* power.

On the other side of the wage spectrum, unions of professional athletes seek liberation from the feudal-like ties which have bound them to employers.

In the 1960s a new public policy asserted a positive line independent of the established pressure groups. The issues of civil rights, manpower, and inflation, representing the fuller development of position public policy, edged the traditional union vs. management questions from the center of the policy arena. Manpower policy as embodied in the series of manpower acts from 1961 on enhanced the interests of both unions and management by (1) increasing worker productivity and mobility through education, training, retraining, and guidance, and by (2) strengthening the institutions of the labor market to achieve a better fit between the structure of supply and the structure of demand. In its early phase manpower policy responded to the immediate urgencies of depressed areas, youth unemployment, technological unemployment, and the competitively disadvantaged. In its later phase manpower policy culminated in the Comprehensive Employment and Training Act (CETA) which sought to establish a "coherent, flexible national manpower policy."

Public policy in the employment aspects of civil rights is embodied mainly in the Civil Rights Act of

1964 and in the President's authority to prescribe standards for federal procurement. Enforced both against management and unions, the policy reflected the impact of a rising pressure group, the civil rights movement. Groups like the NAACP and urban coalitions could bargain with the traditional bargainers over seniority and recruitment of minority entrants. The rising numbers of black workers in unions made them an internal force to contend with.

In its reactive stage, civil rights policy moved to prohibit discrimination in employment. But the reactive policy of no-discrimination proved not to be sufficient in actually bringing together the black worker and the job. The positive phase of civil rights policy is demonstrated in the concepts of "outreach" and "affirmative action" and the restructuring of discriminatory senority systems. These, concepts establish the principle that policy objectives are not fulfilled simply by creating normal market incentives. Incentives alone have, in fact, proved to be inadequate to bring many black workers to the jobs.

Positive public policy appears to assert an unprecedented peacetime concern with the results of collective bargaining and trade unionism. The Norris-LaGuardia, Wagner, Taft-Hartley, and Landrum-Griffin expressions of public policy operated on the theory that the · regulation of the processes of collective bargaining and unionism would be sufficient. Wage-price policy, civil rights, and manpower, by contrast, undertake to define publicly acceptable results of collective bargaining and unionism. The underlying assumption of wage-price policy is that even balanced collective bargaining, left to go its own way, is likely to yield economic results incompatible with a stable price level, a strong balance of payments position, economic growth, and economic recovery. Deflation, incomes policy, wage controls, "jawboning" wage and price freezes are the recurring techniques which the government has used to intervene in collective bargaining with uneven results.

Similarly, the civil rights policy raises the question whether social peace does not require public intervention to protect the interests of minority workers from the discriminatory effects of agreements negotiated by the "white" bargaining parties. Manpower policy weighs results of the union-management relationship at the points of apprenticeship and other training terms which restrict entry in ways inconsistent with public policy interests in freer mobility. The reasoning is that the negotiations between the private parties do not take into sufficient account the social costs of their bargaining results and that intervention is essential to make adjustments congruent with positive public policy.

Positive public policy has by no means displaced pressure group interests. It is rather a case of coexistence. The parties to National Labor Relations Board proceedings perceive Republican appointees to the board as more likely to be employer-leaning in their decisions than are Democratic appointees, and vice versa. Unions engaged in strikes may seek intervention to get themselves off a hook. Employers have lobbied vigorously against stringent enforcement of the Occupational Safety and Health Act of 1970. But the key public policies toward labor of full employment, civil rights, manpower, and wages and prices are as likely to represent an autonomous positive line than a response to pressure group insistence.

The boundaries of positive public policy are being further extended into pension reform and occupational health and safety areas. The Employment Retirement Income Security Act of 1974, better known as the Pension Reform Act, will require a substantial recasting of negotiated pension programs to assure that covered employees will have their promised pension when they retire. Basic to the law are minimum vesting and funding standards designed to assure that a worker who participates in a private pension plan for many years will not lose all pension credits because employment was terminated before retirement or because employer-employee contributions were not adequate to pay the benefits promised.

The Occupational Safety and Health Act is less clear as an example of positive public policy. The unions came to the safety and health campaign relatively late, fearing its negative effect on wages and the supply of jobs. In the management view, OSHA authorizes the most extensive federal intervention in day-to-day plant operations of any previous legislation. Inspectors are authorized to check company compliance with the law, the availability of safety programs including training, and the good faith with which management enforces these programs. The act creates new rights for unions and workers who have to be informed of inspections and violations and the remedial actions taken. In sum, unions and employees have rights in connection with enforcement which they never had before under law. Much of what the

law compels might have been achieved through negotiation in the past if health and safety had been given
a higher priority. "In the past," according to a union
specialist in the field, "the union practice, more often
than not, was to trade and barter its safety and health
demands for a couple of cents an hour in wages." The
consciousness-raising of OSHA has pushed job health
and safety up on the bargaining agenda.

A rank-and-file unrest has permeated the work situation since the early 1960s. This sort of unrest seems
to have been evident in five kinds of settings in this
period: (1) strikes, especially "wildcats," during the
life of an agreement, and other forms of employee
direct action such as slowdowns, mass sick leave, and
sit-ins—much of it in the public sector; (2) eruption
of new union militancy in the public sector; (3) pressures from below for changes in collective bargaining
policies, as in the skilled workers' rebelliousness in the
industrial unions, and contract rejections; (4) pressures from below for a greater say in union affairs, as
evidenced in the defeat of well-established union incumbents—the defeat of David J. McDonald in the
Steelworkers and the end of the John L. Lewis tradition of control with the election of Arnold Miller are
symbolic of this turn of events; and (5) heightened
race consciousness on the shop floor. Strikes during the
term of the agreement (an undetermined proportion
are actually wildcats) represented more than a third of
all the 1960 stoppages, and the percentage has
been rising steadily.

One aspect of rank-and-file unrest goes back to the
"hard line" of the recession of 1957-58 which gave

management the bargaining power to tighten work standards, discipline, and manpower utilization—all perceived as threats to job security. The "hard line" encounter demonstrated the tenacity with which rank and file was ready to fight for job protection when threatened by sudden changes in work rules and technology. It was at this time that observers began to detect a new rank-and-file countervailing power. David Cole called attention, in the spring of 1960, to the "rebelliousness and nonconformance within the labor movement now that we did not see even as recently as five years ago. This is a form of anti-colonialism that the locals are asserting. . . . International unions who recognize the importance of having some orderly procedures for the settlement of these horrible jurisdictional disputes . . . find themselves overruled time and again by their regional and local people."

Economic expansion increased employment and raised employee expectations. The accelerated expansion of public employment provided much of the leverage for the outburst of militancy among public employees. Similarly, employment expansion induced discontent among private-sector workers when they began to measure their earnings against their employers' profits and the rise in the cost of living; and among skilled workers, specifically, who saw their position worsening in respect to both their job inferiors in the shop and their job peers outside. When expansion reached the inflationary stage, unrest arose as protest against wage controls which sought to dampen wage inflation.

Uncertain tendencies in industrial relations fueled shop-floor discontent. Long-term contracts allowed longer periods for maladjustments to build up. Legalistic grievance systems screened complaints too finely, and terms of collective bargaining like health, pensions, and work guarantees became increasingly more difficult for the average union member to grasp. The larger complement of younger workers has been less inclined to put up with established ways in the job and union, especially the seniority system.

Unionism is necessarily a reacting institution; the major initiatives which affect the union lie with the enterprise and the state. The major theme that runs through the 1960s and '70s is the adaptation of collective bargaining and unionism to the increasing demands of public policy and public interests. The state regulates the results as well as the process of collective bargaining at job, industry, and economy levels. Unionism has made great strides in this period. Lessening the tensions incident to employment, it eased the harshness of the hierarchial organization in industry by introducing rights, orderly procedures, and a measure of self-determination at work. It has made feasible higher standards of consumption for working people. Unionism's shock effect has prodded management in general, whether unionized or not, to assume a more human conception of its role and a more efficient management of its labor force.

THE BARGAINING TABLE
by John T. Dunlop

As Professor Barbash has shown, the destiny of the American worker is directly related to that unique U. S. institution—collective bargaining. It is therefore appropriate that the former Secretary of Labor should provide, as a capstone to this chapter, an essay on the evolution of collective bargaining.

The American collective bargaining system embraces at least three characteristics distinctive to industrial relations in the United States. Perhaps the most significant is that our system of industrial relations is highly decentralized. The prevalence of plant and company negotiations grew out of the patterns of organizations among employers and unions scattered across the country. Union and management officials on the local level, being intimately familiar with the issues, were better able to find a position of mutual accommodation. Decentralization has proved to be a great source of strength as it has allowed for greater detail and wider scope in collective bargaining and a much lesser role for substantive governmental rule-making—legislative or administrative.

A second characteristic is the principle of exclusive jurisdiction or representation where one union serves as the sole representative for all employees in the plant or appropriate bargaining unit. In the early days of the union movement, the concurrent existence of the Knights of Labor and the trade unions, both in the same field, resulted in conflict and divided loyalty. Thus, the AFL became devoted to the principle that in each recognized field of activity, there should be but one union, chartered by the AFL. This practice conforms to the American political tradition of electing single representatives by majority vote, and has served to facilitate the bargaining process for both management and workers by requiring employees to choose among competing organizations or no organization, to accommodate competing interests within the union at the bargaining table, and to establish a priority among competing interests in negotiations.

A third characteristic is the role the law plays in the process. Labor law is primarily concerned with the tactics and procedures of organizing, bargaining, and modes of conflict. Substantive terms and conditions of employment are left largely to private negotiation or determination. The law views this as a private responsibility from which the government should stand apart. While governmental regulation in some areas has expanded appreciably in the last two decades—as in equal employment opportunities, safety and pensions—the negotiating parties continue to have wide latitude. Labor and management have been able to determine their own needs for periodic negotiations.

Within the collective bargaining system, gradual change may be expected to continue in at least four areas: the subjects of bargaining; the structure of bargaining; the legal framework of bargaining; and the role of government in the bargaining process. It appears to me unlikely that the preoccupation with job design and work reorganization, attributed to the interests of a younger and better educated work force, will produce major changes in the organization and management of the workplace. Changes relating to flexibility in hours in some industries, greater choice for workers among fringe benefits, and employee participation in the arrangements for work are not, in my view, likely to be extensive. This is because most employees do not appear to be significantly interested, and the number of managements with special interests in these areas is limited.

An area where continuing evolution may be expected relates to the structure of bargaining, that is, the level at which different issues should be resolved; the range of jobs, territory, and employees to be governed by the agreement; and the relations among the different craft unions bargaining with a common employer. Many long and expensive strikes have grown out of disagreements not primarily related to compensation but to the structure of bargaining.

Another area of central issues within the American industrial relations system is whether significant changes in its legal framework can be made through consensus within the system, rather than only through political and legislative conflict as in the past. The legal framework of collective bargaining and many features of the formal operation of collective bargaining reflect artificial and unrealistic legislation. Many of these provisions have been ignored for practical purposes. Some of these issues, such as the structure of collective bargaining itself, the nature of the obligation to bargain, and the status of work rules (so-called featherbedding), are themselves increasingly subjects of collective bargaining. But there exists the possibility that leaders of labor and management may come to develop the means to meet new needs for dispute settlement procedures, changes in the structure of bargaining, and methods to deal even more effectively with the introduction of technological change and with foreign competition. No issue is more important for the future than the procedures through which the legal framework of collective bargaining evolves.

In the past the government's interest in high employment and price stability has resulted in policies that have directly impinged on bargaining. Lloyd Ulman is probably correct in asserting the catnip effect, which suggests "that incomes policy is well-nigh irresistible to politicians in office." Apart from the government's concern with inflation, it is becoming increasingly involved in areas that affect bargaining. The Department of Labor and the states, for example, administer a variety of programs that directly impinge on the relations between bargaining parties. Occupational health and safety, worker's compensation, and equal employment opportunity are obvious examples.

These programs serve constructive ends and will make major contributions to future improvements in the quality of workers' lives. However, there are limits to which we can seek solutions to social and economic problems in terms of legislation and litigation. The challenge for the Department of Labor in the coming years will be to find ways to supplement the law and regulations through consensus and cooperation, and through greater recognition of the interaction between new initiatives and traditional processes such as collective bargaining.

Since 1965 the volume of American imports and exports has more than doubled. This unparalleled growth is likely to have an increasing effect on collective bargaining and industrial relations in general. The greater the interdependence between America and its trading partners, the greater the influence of international factors on domestic bargaining. Among the pressures on the bargaining system will be: the vulnerability of the American economy to political acts abroad and to change in world aggregate demand; the effect of foreign wage rates and labor market policies on domestic employment relations; and the concern that foreign imports are taking American jobs. The move toward freer trade will ultimately benefit the American economy, although some of these transitional pressures will require adaptation by labor and management.

In recent years, there have been frequent attempts to adapt collective bargaining to new areas such as local and state governmental agencies, and health and education institutions. Questions of exclusive jurisdiction, the appropriate subjects for bargaining, and the role of the strike and arbitration have different implications in the public sector than in the private, and will require considerable innovation. It is too early to predict what the end result will be, but it is clear that labor organizations will have a significant impact upon the management and performance of agencies in the public sector and upon nonprofit institutions.

The proliferation of "near-unions" adds a new dimension to collective bargaining. As the American economy and society evolve, it becomes more organized with various groups banding together to advance their interests as they perceive them. Sometimes these groups resemble and act like unions, and at other times they are quite different. Such diverse groups may be cited as women employees, racial minority groups, beef farmers, gasoline dealers, dentists, tenants, and so on. In Southern California an erstwhile man of the cloth has even tried to organize the clergy. The near-unions tend to include supervisory employees as members, who are more dependent, in higher income categories, and in some cases more responsive to professional concerns than are members of conventional unions. Although the total size of near-unions is uncertain, their combined memberships is certainly greater than two million persons. The point is that parties to traditional collective bargaining often have to deal with such groups in the economic and political arenas; sometimes they will directly compete with the bargaining process.

A final area of concern—related tangentially to bargaining—is the interaction between labor organizations and the intellectual community. Particularly in recent years, the relationship between unions and the universities has been strained. Criticisms by liberal intellectuals of labor leaders and labor organizations have widened the gap considerably. The simple fact is that the labor organizations' view of the workers does not comport well with the romanticized view of the intellectual left. Few intellectuals have an accurate sense of how unions work, and consequently have based many of their criticisms on a simplistic understanding of the ability of labor leaders to shape or reflect the sentiments of the rank and file, and this has been a source of friction. The gap is mutually detrimental.

The academic community can offer to unions the same useful interchange that has benefited business, government, and charitable institutions in the United States. Particularly as the issues at the bargaining table become more technical and the relationship between union, management, and government more complex, the intellectual community is in a position to make a constructive contribution towards improving the quality of bargaining.

However, for a rapprochement to occur, intellectuals must acquire a less naive view of the way unions work; it is essential, too, that organized labor take the initiative in searching within higher education for methods of cooperation and points of contact. The American collective bargaining system will continue to live with some tensions. But the system does accommodate and adjust to these conflicts and tensions.

Authors' Biographies

RICHARD B. MORRIS, editor of and contributor to this book, is Gouverneur Morris Professor Emeritus of History at Columbia University, where he has taught for many years, and is current president of the American Historical Association. Professor Morris has lectured abroad, serving as Fulbright Research Professor at the Sorbonne, Distinguished Professor at the John F. Kennedy Institute at the Free University of Berlin, and held the Paley and Truman Foundation Lectureships at the Hebrew University of Jerusalem. He has served on the American Revolution Bicentennial Commission and is currently chairman of the New York State Bicentennial Coordinating Council. Professor Morris has had a longtime commitment to the field of labor history. His *Government and Labor in Early America*, published in 1946, represented a major reexamination of the history of American labor prior to trade unionism. In addition, he has served for some fifteen years as chairman of the Editorial Board of *Labor History*. Professor Morris has also worked in the field of American legal history, American diplomatic history, and the history of the American Revolution. His *Peacemakers: The Great Powers and American Independence* was awarded the Bancroft Prize in 1966. He has recently published *John Jay, The Making of a Revolutionary, 1745-1780,* and is editor of the *Encyclopedia of American History,* the *Bicentennial Edition* of which was published in 1976.

EDWARD PESSEN, author of Chapter 2, is Distinguished Professor of History at Baruch College and the Graduate School and University Center of the City University of New York. Before joining the Infantry in World War II, he worked during the Great Depression as a welder and a metal worker and for a time was a shop steward in the IBEW. His first book, *Most Uncommon Jacksonians: The Radical Leaders of the Early Labor Movement,* was nominated for the Pulitzer Prize in 1968. He has written and edited six additional books, while co-authoring or contributing to twenty-nine others. His *Riches, Class, and Power before Civil War* was a National Book Award finalist in 1974. His more than fifty articles have appeared in the *American Historical Review,* the *Journal of American History,* the *Journal of Urban History, Labor History,* the *Political Science Quarterly, Dissent, The Nation, The New York Times,* the *South Atlantic Quarterly,* and other scholarly journals.

DAVID MONTGOMERY, author of Chapter 3, is a Professor of History at the University of Pittsburgh. After serving in the U.S. Army Corps of Engineers, from which he was discharged as a Staff Sergeant, he studied Political Science at Swarthmore College and graduated with Highest Honors in 1950. For the next ten years he worked as a machinist in New York City and St. Paul, Minnesota, and was active in the United Electrical Workers, the International Association of Machinists, and the Teamsters, as at various times a shop steward, legislative committee member, and local executive board member. While working nights at his trade, he entered graduate school in history at the University of Minnesota in 1959 and received his Ph.D. from that institution in 1962. He is the author of *Beyond Equality: Labor and the Radical Republicans, 1862-1872* and numerous articles on the history of American workers, which have appeared in *Labor History*, the *Journal of Social History*, and *Radical America*.

PHILIP TAFT, author of Chapter 4, was Professor Emeritus at Brown University where he taught from 1937 until his retirement in 1968. He had held visiting professorships at Harvard University, Columbia University, the University of Wisconsin, the University of Michigan, the University of Hawaii, and others. He was the author of numerous books in the field of labor and had been a contributor to the *American Economic Review*, the *Journal of Political Economy*, *Labor History*, *Industrial and Labor Relations Review*, *Harvard Business Review*, *America*, and other periodicals and publications. He had held positions with the Social Security Board and the Resettlement Administration in Washington, D.C. He was a chairman of the New England Trucking Panel of the War Labor Board from 1942-45. He had served as a consultant to the Rhode Island Department of Employment Security and was president of the Industrial Relations Research Association in 1961. He was a member of the Board of Directors of *Labor History* and was a Fellow of the American Academy of Arts and Sciences in 1949. He was the recipient of a John Simon Guggenheim Fellowship in the Bicentennial year. He died in the fall of 1976.

IRVING BERNSTEIN, author of Chapter 5, received his B.A. from the University of Rochester in 1937, his

M.A. from Harvard in 1938, and his Ph.D. from Harvard in 1948. He was a Fellow at the Brookings Institution from 1940-41. He is now Professor of Political Science and Research Associate, Institute of Industrial Relations, University of California, Los Angeles. His early career included positions as an industrial economist at the Bureau of Labor Statistics from 1941-42, a position as hearing officer, National War Labor Board from 1942-43, military service from 1943-45 primarily with the Research and Analysis Branch, Office of Strategic Services, and as chief of the Materials Section, U.S. Conciliation Service from 1946-47. He was also director, Case Analysis Division and chairman, San Francisco Regional Wage Stabilization Board from 1951-52 and has served as arbitrator in numerous labor disputes since 1948. This year he is president of the Industrial Relations Research Association. He is the author of *Turbulent Years: A History of the American Worker, The Lean Years: A History of the American Worker, Arbitration of Wages, The New Deal Collective Bargaining Policy, The Economics of Television Film Production and Distribution, Hollywood at the Crossroads: An Economic Study of the Motion Picture Industry,* and editor-in-chief and contributor to *Emergency Disputes and National Policy.*

JACK BARBASH, author of Chapter 6, is affiliated with the Department of Economics at the University of Wisconsin–Madison. He has been on the faculty since 1957 specializing in industrial relations research, teaching, and consulting. Before that time he served for twenty years as an economist for the National Labor Relations Board, the War Production Board, and U.S. Department of Labor and as staff director for the U. S. Senate Subcommittee on Labor and Labor-

Management Relations. In addition, he has served as an economist for labor unions and as research and education director of the AFL-CIO Industrial Union Department. Professor Barbash is the author of nine books, some of which deal with unions. His latest are *Trade Unions and National Economic Policy (1972)* and *Work in the Changing Society (1975)*. He has also contributed articles to the *American Economic Review, Indusrtial and Labor Relations Review, the British Journal of Industrial Relations and Industrial Relations Research Association,* and numerous other journals and publications and presented papers for annual meetings and for volumes.

JOHN T. DUNLOP, author of the Bargaining Table, served as the nation's fourteenth Secretary of Labor from March 1975 until February 1976. A member of the Harvard University economics faculty since 1938, Dr. Dunlop was chairman of the Harvard Department of Economics from 1961 to 1966 and dean of the Faculty of Arts and Sciences from 1970 to 1973. He is Lamont University Professor presently on leave of absence from Harvard. Dr. Dunlop is the author of a number of books and articles on industrial relations, economics and other subjects and has contributed to numerous other books, articles, and professional journals. He is a member of the National Academy of Arbitrators, the American Academy of Arts and Sciences, and the American Philosophical Society. He was a John Simon Guggenheim Fellow (1952-53), president of the Industrial Relations Research Association (1960), and is currently president of the International Industrial Relations Research Association (1973).

BIBLIOGRAPHY

CHAPTER ONE

Baker, Mary Roys. "Anglo-Massachusetts Trade Union Roots, 1130–1790." *Labor History*, 14, (1973), 352–396.

Ballagh, James C. *White Servitude in the Colony of Virginia*. Baltimore: Johns Hopkins Press, 1895.

Blassingame, John W. *The Slave Community*. New York: Oxford University Press, 1972.

Fogel, Robert W. and Engerman, Stanley L. *Time on the Cross, The Economics of American Negro Slavery*. Boston: Little, Brown & Co., 1974.

Henretta, James A. "Economic Development and Social Structure in Colonial Boston." *William and Mary Quarterly*, 22, (1965), 75–92.

Herrick, Cheesman A. *White Servitude in Pennsylvania*. Philadelphia: J. J. McVey, 1926.

Jernegan, Marcus W. *Laboring and Dependent Classes in Colonial America 1607–1783*. Chicago: University of Chicago Press, 1931.

Jordan, Winthrop D. *White Over Black, American Attitudes Toward the Negro, 1550–1812*. Chapel Hill: University of North Carolina Press, 1968.

Kulikoff, Allan. "The Progress of Inequality in Revolutionary Boston." *William and Mary Quarterly*, 28, (1971), 375–411.

Land, Aubrey C. "Economic Base and Social Structure: The Northern Chesapeake in the Eighteenth Century." *Journal of Economic History*, 25, (1965), 639–654.

Lemisch, Jesse. "Jack Tar in the Streets: Merchant Seamen in the Politics of Revolutionary America." *William and Mary Quarterly*, 25, (1968), 371–407.

Lemisch, Jesse. "Listening to the 'Inarticulate': William Widger's Dream and the Loyalties of American Revolutionary Seamen in British Prisons." *Journal of Social History*, 4, (1971), 333–356.

Lemonxao, James T. and Nash, Gary B. "The Distribution of

Wealth in Eighteenth Century America: A Century of Changes in Chester County, Pennsylvania, 1693–1802." *Journal of Social History*, 2, (1968–69), 9–12.

Lynd, Staughton. "The Mechanics in New York Politics, 1774–1788." *Labor History*, 5, (1968), 225–246.

Maier, Pauline. From Resistance to Revolution. New York: Alfred A. Knopf, 1972.

Main, Jackson T. *The Social Structure of Revolutionary America*. Princeton: Princeton University Press, 1965.

McCormac, Eugene I. *White Servitude in Maryland, 1634–1820*. Baltimore: Johns Hopkins Press, 1904.

Mohl, Raymond A. *Poverty in New York, 1783–1825*. New York: Oxford University Press, 1931.

Morris, Richard B., ed. *The Era of the American Revolution*. New York: Columbia University Press, 1939.

Morris, Richard B. *Government and Labor in Early America*. New York: Columbia University Press, 1946.

Morris, Richard B. "The Measure of Bondage in the Slave States." *Mississippi Valley Historical Review*, 41, (1954), 219–240.

Seybolt, Robert F. *Apprenticeship and Apprenticeship Education in Colonial New England and New York*. New York: Columbia University Press, 1971.

Smith, Abbot Emerson. *Colonists in Bondage: White Servitude and Convict Labor in America, 1607–1776*. Chapel Hill: University of North Carolina Press, 1947.

Smith, Warren B. *White Servitude in Colonial South Carolina*. Columbia: University of South Carolina Press, 1961.

Starobin, Robert S. *Industrial Slavery in the Old South*. New York: Oxford University Press, 1970.

Towner, Lawrence W. "A Fondness for Freedom, Servant Protest in Puritan Society." *William and Mary Quarterly*, 19, (1962), 201–219.

Walsh, Richard. *Charleston's Sons of Liberty*. Columbia: University of South Carolina Press, 1959.

Wood, Peter H. *Black Majority: Negroes in Colonial South Carolina from 1670 through the Stono Rebellion*. New York: Alfred A. Knopf, 1974.

Young, Alfred F. *The Democratic Republicans of New York, The Origins, 1763–1797*. Chapel Hill: University of North Carolina Press, 1967.

CHAPTER TWO

Adams, Donald R., Jr. "Some Evidence on English and American Wage Rates, 1790–1830." *Journal of Economic History*, 30, (1970), 499–513.

Adams, Donald R., Jr. "Wage Rates in the Early National Period." *Journal of Economic History*, 28 (1968), 404–426.

Arky, Louis. "The Mechanics' Union of Trade Associations and the Formation of the Philadelphia Working Men's Movement." *Pennsylvania Magazine of History and Biography*, 76, (1952), 142–176.

Burn, James D. *Three Years Among the Working Classes in the United States during the War*. London: Smith, Elder & Co., 1865.

Commons, John R., ed. *A Documentary History of American Industrial Society*. 10 Vols. Cleveland: A. H. Clark, 1910.

Commons, John R., *et al*. *History of Labour in the United States*. Vols. I and II. New York: Macmillan, 1918.

Dew, Charles B. "Disciplining Slave Ironworkers in the Antebellum South: Coercion, Conciliation and Accommodation." *American Historical Review*, 79, (1974), 393–418.

Faler, Paul. "Cultural Aspects of the Industrial Revolution; Lynn, Massachusetts Shoemakers and Industrial Morality, 1826–1860." *Labor History*, 15, (1974), 367–394.

Gitelman, Howard M. "The Waltham System and the Coming of the Irish." *Labor History*, 8, (1967), 227–253.

Grossman, Jonathan. *William Sylvis, Pioneer of American Labor: A Study of the Labor Movement During the Era of the Civil War*. New York: Columbia University Press, 1945.

Gutman, Herbert G. "Work, Culture and Society in Industrializing America, 1815–1919." *American History Review*, 78, (1973), 531–588.

Hugins, Walter. *Jacksonian Democracy and the Working Class*. Stanford: Stanford University Press, 1960.

Josephson, Hannah. *The Golden Threads*. New York: Duell, Sloan & Pearce, 1949.

Laurie, Bruce. " 'Nothing on Impulse': Life Styles of Philadelphia Artisans, 1820–1860." *Labor History*, 15, (1974), 337–366.

Lebergott, Stanley. *Manpower in Economic Growth*. New York: McGraw-Hill, 1964.

Lebergott, Stanley. *Trends in the American Economy in the 19th Century*. Princeton: Princeton University Press, 1960.

Modell, John. "The Peopling of a Working Class Ward: Reading, Pa., 1950." *Journal of Social History*, 5, (1971).

Montgomery, David. *Beyond Equality: Labor and the Radical Republicans*. New York: Alfred A. Knopf, 1967.

Montgomery, David. "The Shuttle and the Cross: Weavers and Artisans in the Kensington Riots of 1844." *Journal of Social History*, 5, (1972), 411–446.

Morris, Richard B. "Andrew Jackson, Strikebreaker." *American Historical Review*, 55, (1949), 54–68.

Morris, Richard B. "The Course of Peonage in a Slave State." *Political Science Quarterly*, 65, (1950), 238–262.

Morris, Richard B. "Criminal Conspiracy and Early Labor Combinations in New York." *Political Science Quarterly*, 57, (1937), 51–85.

Morris, Richard B. "Labor Controls in Maryland in the 19th Century." *Journal of Southern History*, 14, (1948), 385–400.

Morris, Richard B. "The Measure of Bondage in the Slave States." *Mississippi Valley Historical Review*, 41, (1954), 219–240.

Nelles, Walter. "The First American Labor Case." *Yale Law Journal*, 41, (1931).

Pessen, Edward. *Jacksonian America*. Homewood: Dorsey Press, 1969.

Pessen, Edward. *Most Uncommon Jacksonians: The Radical Leaders of the Early Labor Movement*. Albany: State University of New York Press, 1967.

Pessen, Edward. "The Working Men's Movement of the Jacksonian Era." *Mississippi Valley Historical Review*, 43, (1956), 428–443.

Pessen, Edward. "The Working Men's Party Revisited." *Labor History*, 4, (1963), 203–226.

Rosenberg, Walter. "Anglo-American Wage Differences in the 1820's." *Journal of Economic History*, 27, (1967), 221–229.

Schlesinger, Arthur M., Jr. *The Age of Jackson*. Boston: Little, Brown & Co., 1945.

Shlakman, Vera. *Economic History of a Factory Town: A Study of Chicopee, Massachusetts*. Northampton: Smith College, Department of History, 1934.

Starobin, Robert S. *Industrial Slavery in the Old South*. New York: Oxford University Press, 1970.

Sullivan, William A. "Did Labor Support Andrew Jackson?" *Political Science Quarterly*, 62, (1947), 569–580.

Sullivan, William A. *The Industrial Worker in Pennsylvania 1800–1840*. Harrisburg: Pennsylvania Historical and Museum Commission, 1955.

Tyron, Rolla M. *Household Manufactures in the United States 1640–1860*. Chicago: University of Chicago Press, 1917.

Ware, Caroline. *The Early New England Cotton Manufactures*. Boston: Hart, Schraffner & Mark, 1931.

Ware, Norman. *The Industrial Worker 1840–1860*. Boston: Houghton Mifflin, 1924.

Young, Alfred. "The Mechanics and the Jeffersonians." *Labor History*, 5, (1964), 274–276.

CHAPTER THREE

Bernstein, Samuel. *The First International in America.* New York: Augustus M. Kelley, 1962.

Berthoff, Rowland. "The Social Order of the Anthracite Region, 1825–1902." *Pennsylvania Magazine of History and Biography,* 79, (1965).

Bisno, Abraham. *Abraham Bisno, Union Pioneer.* Madison: University of Wisconsin Press, 1967.

Bodner, John, ed. *The Ethnic Experience in Pennsylvania.* Lewisburg: Bucknell University Press, 1973.

Brecher, Jeremy. *Strike!* San Francisco: Straight Arrow Books, 1972.

Broehl, Wayne. *The Molly Maguires.* Cambridge: Harvard University Press, 1964.

Cahan, Abraham. *The Rise of David Levinsky.* New York: Harper &. Brothers, 1917.

Commons, John R., *et al. History of Labour in the United States.* Vols. I and II. New York: Macmillan, 1962.

David, Henry. *The History of the Haymarket Affair.* New York: Russell & Russell, 1936.

Fitch, John A. *The Steel Workers.* New York: Russell Sage Foundation, 1911.

Foner, Philip S. *History of the Labor Movement in the United States.* New York: International Publishers, 1955.

Foner, Philip S. *Organized Labor and the Black Worker, 1619–1973.* New York: Praeger Publishers, 1974.

Galster, Augusta E. *The Labor Movement in the Shoe Industry, with Special Reference to Philadelphia.* New York: Ronald Press, 1924.

Ginger, Ray. *The Binding Cross: A Biography of Eugene Victor Debs.* New Brunswick: Rutgers University Press, 1949.

Gompers, Samuel. *Seventy Years of Life and Labor.* New York: E.P. Dutton & Co., 1925.

Gould, E.R.L. *The Social Condition of Labor.* Baltimore: Johns Hopkins Press, 1893.

Greene, Victor R. *The Slavic Community on Strike: Immigrant Labor in Pennsylvania Anthracite.* Notre Dame: University of Notre Dame Press. 1968.

Grob, Gerald N. *Workers and Utopia: A Study of Ideological Conflict in the American Labor Movement, 1865–1900.* Evanston: Northwestern University Press, 1961.

Gutman, Herbert G., ed. *Work, Culture and Society in Industrializing America.* New York: Alfred A. Knopf, 1976.

Handlin, Oscar. *The Uprooted: The Epic Story of the Great Migrations That Made the American People.* Boston: Little, Brown & Co., 1951.

Harvey, Katherine A. *The Best-Dressed Miners: Life and Labor* in the Maryland Coal Region, 1835–1910. Ithaca: Cornell University Press, 1969.

Hutchinson, E.P. *Immigrants and Their Children, 1850–1950*. New York: John Wiley & Sons, 1956.

Jacobson, Julius, ed. *The Negro and the American Labor Movement*. New York: Doubleday & Co., 1968.

Kirkland, Edward C. *Dream and Thought in the Business Community*. Ithaca: Cornell University Press, 1956.

Kirkland, Edward C. *Industry Comes of Age: Business, Labor and Public Policy, 1860–1897*. New York: Holt, Rinehart & Winston, 1961.

Kleinberg, Susan J. "Technology and Women's Work: The Lives of Working Class Women in Pittsburgh, 1870–1900." *Labor History*, 17, (1976), 58–72.

Kleppner, Paul. *The Cross of Culture: A Social Analysis of Midwestern Politics, 1850–1900*. New York: Free Press, 1970.

Laurie, Bruce, Herschberg, Theodore and Alter, George. "Immigrants and Social History: The Philadelphia Experience, 1850–1880." *Journal of Social History*, 9, (1976), 219–267.

Lebergott, Stanley. *Manpower in Economic Growth*. New York: McGraw-Hill, 1964.

McLauren, Melton A. *Paternalism and Protest: Southern Cotton Mill Workers and Organized Labor, 1875–1905*. Westport: Greenwood Publishing Corp., 1971.

McNeill, George E., ed. *The Labor Movement: The Problem of To-Day*. New York: M.W. Hazen, 1887.

Moller, Herbert, ed. *Population Movements in Modern European History*. New York: Macmillan, 1964.

Montgomery, David. *Beyond Equality: Labor and the Radical Republicans, 1862–1872*. New York: Alfred A. Knopf, 1967.

Nee, Victor and DeBarry, Brett. *Longtime Californ'*. New York: Pantheon Press, 1972.

North, Douglass C. *Growth and Welfare in the American Past: A New Economic History*. Englewood Cliffs: Prentice-Hall, 1966.

Ozanne, Robert. *A Century of Labor-Management Relations at McCormick and International Harvester*. Madison: University of Wisconsin Press, 1967.

Powderly, Terence V. *Thirty Years of Labor, 1859–1889*. Columbus: Excelsior Publishing House, 1889.

Quint, Howard. *The Forging of American Socialism*. Indianapolis: Bobbs-Merrill, 1953.

Report of the Committee of the Senate upon the Relations between Labor and Capital. Washington: Government Printing Office, 1885.

Saxton, Alexander. *The Indispensable Enemy: Labor and the Anti-Chinese Movement in California.* Berkeley: University of California Press, 1971.

Spero, Sterling D. and Harris, Abram L. *The Black Worker: The Negro and the Labor Movement.* New York: Columbia University Press, 1931.

Thomas, Brinley. *Migration and Economic Growth: A Study of Great Britain and the Atlantic Economy.* Cambridge: University Press, 1954.

U.S. Bureau of the Census. *Historical Statistics of the United States, Colonial Times to 1957.* Washington. Government Printing Office, 1960.

Van Tine, Warren R. *The Making of a Labor Bureaucrat: Union Leadership in the United States, 1870–1920.* Amherst: University of Massachusetts Press, 1973.

Ware, Norman. *The Labor Movement in the United States, 1860–1895.* New York: Appleton, 1929.

Worthman, Paul B. "Black Workers and Labor Unions in Birmingham, Alabama, 1897–1904." *Labor History,* 10, (1969).

Yearly, Clifton K., Jr. *Britons in American Labor.* Baltimore: Johns Hopkins Press, 1957.

Yellen, Samuel. *American Labor Struggles.* New York: Harcourt, Brace & Co., 1936.

CHAPTER FOUR

Adkins v. *Children's Hospital,* 226 United States 525 (1923).

American Steel Foundries v. *Tri-Central Trades Council,* 27 United States 184 (1921).

Angel, Paul. *Bloody Williamson.* New York: Alfred A. Knopf, 1952.

Bailey v. *Drexel Furniture Company,* 259 United States 20 (1922).

Baltimore and Ohio Railroad Co. v. *International Commerce Commission,* 221 United States 621 (1911).

Bedford Cut Stone Co. v. *Journeymen Stone Cutters' Association,* 275 United States 37 (1927).

Bing, Alexander. *War Time Strikes and Their Adjustment.* New York: E. P. Dutton, 1921.

Bonnet, Clarence E. *Employer Associations in the United States.* New York: Macmillan, 1928.

Buck's Stove and Range Co. v. *American Federation of Labor* 221 United States 418 (1911), 223 United States 604 (1914).

Bunting v. *Oregon,* 243 United States 426 (1916).

Connell, Robert J. *The Anthracite Coal Strike of 1902.* Washington: Catholic University Press, 1957.

Coppage v. *Kansas*, 236 United States 1 (1915).

Douglas, Paul H. *Real Wages in the United States, 1890–1926.* New York: Houghton Mifflin, 1930.

Duplex Printing Press Co. v. *Deering*, 254 United States 469 (1921).

Foster, William Z. *The Great Steel Strike.* New York: B.V. Huebsch, 1920.

Grant, Luke. *The National Erectors Association and the International Association of Bridge and Iron Workers.* Washington: Chicago, Barnard & Miller Print. 1915.

Harding, Alfred. *The Revolt of the Actors.* New York: William Morrow, 1929.

Hawkins v. *Blakley*, 243 United States 212 (1917).

Hitchman Coal and Coke Co. v. *Mitchell*, 245 United States 245 (1917).

Hoagland, Henry. *Wage Bargaining on the Vessels of the Great Lakes.* Urbana: University of Illinois Press, 1917.

Holden v. *Hardy*, 169 United States 336 (1898).

Hoxie, Robert. *Trade Unionism in the United States.* New York: Macmillan, 1928.

Jensen, Vernon H. *Heritage of Conflict.* Ithaca: Cornell University Press, 1950.

Lane, Winthrop D. *Civil War in West Virginia.* New York: B. V. Huebsch, 1921.

Leiserson, William M. *Adjusting Immigrant and Industry.* New York: Harper & Brothers, 1924.

Levine, Louis. *The Women's Garment Workers.* New York: B. V. Huebsch, 1924.

Lochner v. *New York*, 198 United States 45 (1904).

Mountain Timber v. *Washington*, 243 United States 238 (1917).

New York Railroad Co. v. *White*, 243 United States 188 (1917).

Perlman, Selig and Taft, Philip. *History of Labor in the United States, 1896–1932.* New York: Macmillan, 1935.

Rastall, Benjamin. "The Labor History of the Cripple Creek District." *University of Wisconsin Press Bulletin*, 198, (1908).

Rees, Albert. *Real Earnings in Manufacturing.* Princeton: Princeton University Press, 1961.

Report of the Industrial Commission on the Chicago Labor Disputes of 1900. Vol. III. Washington: Government Printing Office, 1902.

Taft, Philip. *The A.F. of L. in the Time of Gompers.* New York: Harper & Brothers, 1957.

Taft, Philip. *Organized Labor in American History.* New York: Harper & Row, 1964.

Taft, Philip. "On the Origins of Business Unionism." *Industrial and Labor Relations Review*, October, 1963.

Texas v. *New Orleans Railroad Co.* v. *Brotherhood*, 281 United States 543 (1930).

United States Commission of Industrial Relations. Washington: Government Printing Office, 1915.

Washington, Booker T. "The Negro and the Labor Unions." *Atlantic Monthly*, June, 1913.

West, George P. "Report on the Colorado Strike." *Committee on Industrial Relations*, Washington, 1915.

Wilson v. *New*, 243 United States (1817).

Witte, Edwin W. *The Government in Labor Disputes*. New York: McGraw-Hill, 1932.

Wolman, Leo. *Ebb and Flow in Trade Unionism*. New York: National Bureau of Economic Research, 1936.

CHAPTER FIVE

Altmeyer, Arthur J. *The Formative Years of Social Security*. Madison: University of Wisconsin Press, 1966.

Bernstein, Irving. *The Lean Years*. Boston: Houghton Mifflin, 1960.

Bernstein, Irving. *The New Deal Collective Bargaining Policy*. Berkeley: University of California Press, 1950.

Bernstein, Irving. *Turbulent Years*. Boston: Houghton Mifflin, 1970.

Brown, Josephine C. *Public Relief, 1929–1939*. New York: Holt, 1940.

Charles, Searle F. *Minister of Relief, Harry Hopkins and the Depression*. Syracuse: Syracuse University Press, 1963.

Derber, Milton and Young, Edwin, eds. *Labor and the New Deal*. Madison: University of Wisconsin Press, 1957.

Douglas, Paul A. *Social Security in the United States*. New York: Whittlesey House, 1936.

Epstein, Abraham. *Insecurity: A Challenge to America*. New York: Smith & Haas, 1933.

Galenson, Walter. *The CIO Challenge to the AFL: A History of the American Labor Movement, 1935–1941*. Cambridge: Harvard University Press, 1960.

Howard, Donald S. *The WPA and Federal Relief Policy*. New York: Russell Sage Foundation, 1943.

Lubove, Roy. *The Struggle for Social Security, 1900–1935*. Cambridge: Harvard University Press, 1968.

MacMahon, Arthur W., Millet, John D., and Ogden, Gladys. *The Administration of Federal Work Relief*. Chicago: Public Administration Service, 1941.

Morris, James O. *Conflict Within the AFL: A Study of Craft Versus Industrial Unionism, 1901–1938.* Ithaca: Cornell University Press, 1958.

Nathan, Robert R. "Estimates of Unemployment in the United States." *International Labour Review,* 63, (January, 1936), 49–73.

Schlesinger, Arthur M., Jr. *The Coming of the New Deal.* Boston: Houghton Mifflin, 1959.

Seidman, Joel. *American Labor from Defense to Reconversion.* Chicago: University of Chicago Press, 1953.

Taft, Philip. *The A.F.L. From the Death of Gompers to the Merger.* New York: Harper, 1959.

Terkel, Studs. *Hard Times, An Oral History of the Great Depression.* New York: Pantheon Press, 1970.

U.S. Department of Commerce, Bureau of the Census. *Historical Statistics of the United States, Colonial Times to 1957.* Washington: Government Printing Office, 1960.

U.S. Department of Labor, Bureau of Labor Statistics. *Report on the Work of the National Defense Mediation Board, March 19, 1941 — January 12, 1942.* Bulletin 714. Washington: Government Printing Office, 1948.

United States National War Labor Board. *The Termination Report of the National War Labor Board: Industrial Disputes and Wage Stabilization in Wartime.* 3 Vols. Washington: Government Printing Office, 1948.

Witte, Edwin E. *The Development of the Social Security Act.* Madison: University of Wisconsin Press, 1962.

CHAPTER SIX

Ashenfelter, Orley and Rees, Albert, eds. *Discrimination in Labor Markets.* Princeton: Princeton University Press, 1973.

Ashford, Nicholas A. *Crisis in the Work Place.* Cambridge: MIT Press, 1976.

Barbash, Jack. *American Unions: Government, Structure and Politics.* New York: Random House, 1967.

Barbash, Jack. "The Strike Wave." *The New Leader,* March 30, 1946.

Bok, Derek C. and Dunlop, John T. *Labor and the American Community.* New York: Simon & Schuster, 1970.

Cormier, Frank and Eaton, William J. *Reuther.* Englewood Cliffs: Prentice-Hall, 1970.

Cox, Archibald. *Law and the National Labor Policy.* Los Angeles: University of California Press, 1960.

Dunlop, John T., ed. *Automation and Technological Change.* Englewood Cliffs: Prentice-Hall, 1962.

Estey, Marten S., Taft, Philip and Wagner, Martin, eds. *Regulating Government*. New York: Harper & Row, 1964.

Fleming, R.W. *The Labor Arbitration Process*. Urbana: University of Illinois Press, 1965.

Goldberg, Arthur J. *AFL-CIO, Labor United*. New York: McGraw-Hill, 1956.

Goulden, Joseph C. *Meany*. New York: Atheneum, 1972.

Hutchinson, John. *The Imperfect Union*. New York: E.P. Dutton & Co., 1970.

Kuhn, James W. *Bargaining in Grievance Settlement*. New York: Columbia University Press, 1961.

Raskin, A.H. "Shanker's Great Leap." The *New York Times Magazine*, September 9, 1973.

Rowan, Richard, ed. *Collective Bargaining Survival in the 1970's*. Philadelphia: Wharton School, University of Pennsylvania, 1973.

Shapiro, Fred C. "How Jerry Wurf Walks on Water." The *New York Times Magazine*, April 11, 1976.

Slichter, Sumner, Healy, James J. and Livernash, Robert E. *The Impact of Collective Bargaining on Management*. Washington: Brookings Institution, 1960.

Spero, Sterling and Capozzola, John M. *The Urban Community and Its Unionized Bureauracies*. New York: Dunelleu, 1973.

Taft, Philip. *Corruption and Racketeering in the Labor Movement*. Ithaca: Cornell University Press, 1970.

Taylor, Ronald B. *Chavez and the Farm Workers*. Boston: Beacon Press, 1975.

U.S. Department of Health, Education and Welfare. *Work in America*. Cambridge: MIT Press, 1973.

U.S. Department of Labor, Bureau of Labor Statistics. *Directory of National Unions and Employee Associations, 1973*. Washington: Government Printing Office, 1974.

Zagora, Sam, ed. *Public Workers and Public Unions*. Englewood Cliffs: Prentice-Hall (Spectrum), 1972.

GLOSSARY

AGENCY SHOP: A union security clause whereby all members of a bargaining unit must pay a service fee, the equivalent of dues, whether or not they are union members.

AMERICAN PLAN: A post-World War I employer movement which stressed freedom of industry to manage its business without union interference.

APPRENTICE: An individual in training for a skilled trade.

ARBITRATION: The referral of collective bargaining or grievance disputes to an impartial third party. Usually the arbitrator's decision is final and binding, although there is "advisory arbitration" in which the decision of the arbitrator is taken under advisement by the parties.

AUTOMATION: Self-correcting feedback and computer electronics. Also, dramatic technological innovation of any sort at the workplace. Often regarded by unions as a cause of unemployment, job alienation, and dislocation.

BARGAINING UNIT: A specified group of employees empowered to bargain collectively with their employer.

BLUE-COLLAR WORKERS: Those in private and public employment who engage in manual labor or the skilled trades.

BOYCOTT: The term originated in 1880 when an Irish landowner, Captain Charles Boycott, was denied all services. Today the expression means collective pressure on employers by refusal to buy their goods or services.

BREAD-AND-BUTTER UNIONISM: Also called "business unionism" or "pure-and-simple unionism." Adolph Strasser, president of the Cigar Makers Union and one of the founders of the AFL, once told a Congressional Committee: "We have no ultimate ends. We are going from day to day. We fight only for immediate objectives—objectives that will be realized in a few years—we are all practical men."

CENTRAL LABOR COUNCIL: A city or county federation of local unions which are affiliated with different national or international unions.

CHECKOFF: A clause in union contract authorizing the employer to deduct dues or service fees from employees' paychecks and remit them to the union.

CLOSED SHOP: The hiring and employment of union members only. Illegal under the Taft-Hartley Act.

COLLECTIVE BARGAINING: The determination of wages and other conditions of employment by direct negotiations between the union and employer.

COMPANY STORE: A store operated by a company for its employees. Often prices were higher here than elsewhere. Occasionally, workers were paid in script redeemable only at the company store.

COMPANY UNION: An employee association organized, controlled, and financed by the employer. Outlawed by the National Labor Relations Act.

CONCILIATION: An attempt by an impartial third party to reconcile differences between labor and management.

CONSPIRACY CASES: The Philadelphia cordwainers' case in 1806 and subsequent decisions involving labor disputes declared unions to be unlawful conspiracies. In 1842 the court decision in *Commonwealth v. Hunt* said that under certain circumstances unions were lawful.

CONSULTATION: Clauses in union contracts or in some state laws applicable to public employees stating that management must consult the union before making any major personnel changes.

CONTRACT LABOR: Workers signed a contract in Colonial times making them indentured servants for the life of the agreement. The system was later used to import Orientals into California and Hawaii and Italians and Greeks for work on the East Coast. It was bitterly fought by organized labor for the contract worker meant low wage competition.

COOPERATIVE STORE: A nonprofit store that is collectively owned and operated for the benefit of both the seller and the shopper.

COST-OF-LIVING INDEX: The Consumer Price Index prepared by the U.S. Bureau of Labor Statistics. The Index measures changes in the cost of living month by month, year by year.

CRAFT UNIONS: Trade unions organized along lines of their

skilled crafts. They formed the base of the American Federation of Labor.

CRIMINAL SYNDICALISM: Syndicalism comes from the French word for union—"syndicat." Syndicalists believe unions should run the economy. The term is associated with the Industrial Workers of the World. Half the states just after World War I passed criminal syndicalist laws. In California a person could be convicted for having once belonged to the IWW. In New Mexico, an employer could be prosecuted for hiring an "anarchist."

DAYWORK: The worker is paid a fixed amount for the day rather than being paid a salary or being paid for the individual piece produced.

DISCRIMINATION: Unequal treatment of workers because of race, sex, religion, nationality, or union membership.

DUAL-UNIONISM: The AFL expelled most CIO unions in 1937 for dual unionism because industrial unions were encroaching on the jurisdiction of craft unions within factories.

ESCALATOR CLAUSE: A clause in the union contract which provides for a cost-of-living increase in wages by relating wages to changes in consumer prices. Usually the Consumer Price Index is used as the measure of price changes.

EXECUTIVE ORDER 10988: President John F. Kennedy issued this Executive Order which recognized the right of federal employees to bargain with management.

FAIR LABOR STANDARDS ACT: Passed in 1938, this law set minimum wages and overtime rates and prohibited child labor for industry connected with interstate commerce.

FALL RIVER SYSTEM: The factory system which employed men, women, and children and made no special provisions for their housing.

FEATHERBEDDING: Employing more workers than are actually necessary to complete a task.

FREE RIDER: A worker in the bargaining unit who refuses to join the union but accepts all the benefits negotiated by the union. Also called a "freeloader."

FRIENDLY SOCIETIES: Early labor groups formed by workers for social and philanthropic purposes.

FRINGE BENEFITS: Negotiated gains other than wages such as vacations, holidays, pensions, insurance and supplemental unemployment benefits.

FULL EMPLOYMENT ACT: Passed in 1946 by a Congress which intended to establish machinery to maintain full employment. A Council of Economic Advisers was created to survey the status of the American economy and to advise the President. The Act, however, failed to solve the unemployment problem.

GAG ORDER: President Theodore Roosevelt issued an executive order dubbed by unions "the gag order" which forbade federal employees on pain of dismissal to seek legislation on their behalf except through their own department.

GOON: A person brought in from the outside to break strikes and union-organizing attempts.

GOVERNMENT BY INJUNCTION: The use of the injunction by government to break strikes.

GREENBACKISM: Reference to partisans of the Greenback Party and the Greenback Labor Party of the 1870s. Greenbackers advocated increased issues of paper money to make cash more readily available to people. They also demanded shorter work hours, abolition of convict labor, boards of labor statistics, and restrictions on immigrant labor.

GRIEVANCE COMMITTEE: A committee within the local union which processes grievances arising from the violation of the contract, state or federal law, or an abuse of a shop's past practice.

GROG PRIVILEGES: The practice of allowing laborers to stop work and have an afternoon drink.

HANDICRAFT SYSTEM: A pre-industrial system where the skilled artisan found identity, pride, and self-worth in his work.

HOT CARGO: A clause in a union contract which says that workers cannot be compelled to handle goods from an employer involved in a strike.

IMPRESSMENT: The act of forcing American seamen into the service of the British Navy.

IMPROVEMENT FACTOR: An annual wage increase negotiated by the union and management which recognizes that the rising productivity of workers contributes to the company's profitability.

INCENTIVE PAY: A system based on the amount of production turned out by workers.

INDENTURED SERVANT: A person bound through a contract to the service of another for a specified amount of time.

INDUSTRIAL DEMOCRACY: A phrase once used to describe unions

as a humanizing force at the workplace. In the 1970s it is coming to mean worker participation in management decision-making.

INDUSTRIAL REVOLUTION: The great advances in technology beginning in the late eighteenth century turned America from a handicraft economy into one of technological mass production.

INDUSTRIAL UNION: A union which includes all the workers in an industry regardless of their craft. Industrial unions formed the base of the CIO.

INJUNCTION: A court order which prohibits a party from taking a particular course of action, such as picketing in the case of a union on strike.

INTERNATIONAL UNION: A union with members in both the United States and Canada.

JOURNEYMAN: A worker who has completed his apprenticeship in a trade or craft and is therefore considered a qualified skilled worker.

JURISDICTIONAL DISPUTES: Arguments among unions over which union represents workers at a job site.

LANDRUM-GRIFFIN ACT: The Labor-Management Reporting and Disclosure Act of 1959. The law contains regulations for union election procedures and supervision of their financial affairs by the U. S. Department of Labor.

LITTLE STEEL FORMULA: The World War II War Labor Board introduced the "Little Steel formula" which tied the cost of living to wage increases "as a stabilization factor."

LOCKOUT: When an employer closes down the factory in order to coerce workers into meeting his demands or modifying their demands.

LOWELL SYSTEM: The system associated with Lowell, Massachusetts, whereby workers, mainly young women, lived in boarding houses owned and run by the company.

MAINTENANCE OF MEMBERSHIP: A provision in the union contract which says that a worker who voluntarily joins the union must remain a member for the duration of the agreement.

MASSACRE: Union descriptions of tragic events in labor history. Examples include Chicago's Memorial Day Massacre where ten steelworkers were shot dead and over eighty were wounded by police on May 30, 1937. There was the Hilo, Hawaii, Massacre of 1938 where nearly fifty unionists were shot or bayonetted by police while sitting on a government pier protesting the unloading of a struck ship. Also, the Ludlow Massacre of 1914 which included the killing of eleven children and two women by the state militia.

MAY DAY: In 1889 the International Socialist Congress meeting in Paris fixed May 1 as the day to publicize the eight-hour day because America's AFL was going to hold an eight-hour-day demonstration on May 1, 1890. Since that time May Day has become a major celebration in communist countries. President Eisenhower in 1955 proclaimed May 1 as "Loyalty Day."

MECHANICS INSTITUTES: A workers' education movement for self-improvement in the 1830s and '40s.

MEDIATION: Attempts by an impartial third party to get labor and management to find agreement during a dispute.

MERIT SYSTEM: The major grievance of public employees was the indignity and insecurity fostered by the political patronage system which ruled government employment. They wanted a system where they would be hired and promoted on their merit. The merit system was introduced by passage of the Civil Service Act of 1883.

MINIMUM WAGE: The lowest rate of pay an employer is allowed to pay under the law or a union contract.

MODIFIED UNION SHOP: A provision in the union contract requiring all new employees to join the union and requiring all workers already in the union to remain as union members.

MOHAWK VALLEY FORMULA: Developed by James Rand, president of Remington Rand, in 1936 to break strikes. The formula included discrediting union leaders by calling them "agitators," threatening to move the plant, raising the banner of "law and order" to mobilize the community against the union, and actively engaging police in strike-breaking activity, then organizing a back-to-work movement of pro-company employees. While the National Association of Manufacturers enthusiastically published the plan, the National Labor Relations Board called it a battle plan for industrial war.

MOLLY MAGUIRES: A group of Irish miners who in the 1860s and '70s vandalized the mines and terrorized the bosses. Ten were hanged as the leaders of the conspiracy after Pinkerton agent, James McParland, exposed them in 1877.

MOONLIGHTING: Working more than one job.

NATIONAL LABOR RELATIONS ACT OF 1935: Also known as the "Wagner Act" after the law's chief sponsor, Senator Robert

Wagner of New York. It represented a fundamental turnaround in government's attitudes toward labor relations. The law created a National Labor Relations Board to carry out its goals of guaranteeing the right of workers to form unions of their own choosing and to bargain collectively with employers.

ONE BIG UNION: The slogan of the IWW which stressed the inclusion of everyone, regardless of trade, into an all-encompassing union. This was also the rationale for the general strike where workers in all type of employment would strike at the same time.

OPEN SHOP: A business that employs workers without regard to union membership. In the 1920s the "open shop" employed an ill-disguised attempt to get ride of bona fide unions. States with "Right to Work" laws have decreed the open shop.

PACE-SETTER: A method of speeding up work. The pace-setter is a person who sets the work pace, usually at an ever higher rate, by leading the work gang and necessitating its catching up with him.

PALMER RAIDS: In 1919-20, U.S. Attorney General A. Mitchell Palmer conducted raids on the headquarters of alleged radicals. Unionists, liberals, radicals, and aliens were indiscriminately arrested and around four thousand were tried for their dissent from the status quo with little regard for their civil rights.

PATERNALISM: The company considered itself the father of its employees and as such had the responsibility of regulating their lives through company houses, stores, hospitals, theaters, sports programs, churches, publications, and codes of behavior on and off the job. Paternalism was also prevalent in public employment. Teachers in 1915 were not permitted to marry, keep company with men, travel beyond the city limits, smoke, dress in bright colors, or wear skirts shorter than two inches above the ankles.

PERB: The abbreviation of state public employment relations boards.

PERQUISITES: In addition to payment of wages, the company provided employees with room, board, and medical care.

PICKETING: The stationing of persons outside a place of employment to publically protest the employer and to discourage entry of nonstriking workers or customers. Most picketing takes place during strikes although there is also informational picketing conducted against nonunion business establishments.

PIECEWORK: The incentive wage system by which workers are paid by the individual piece worked on or completed.

248 ★ A History of the American Worker

PINKERTONS: Agents of the Allan Pinkerton Detective Agency of Chicago who were hired by employers to break strikes or act as company spies within unions. Some believe the expression "Fink," a pejorative term for a worker not loyal to the union, originated by combining a common expletive with the word "Pinkerton."

POLITICAL ACTION: Unions engaged in political action at least as far back as the 1820s, when they demanded universal free public education and abolition of imprisonment for debt as their major social reform issues. Today, AFL-CIO and independent unions expend a substantial amount of money and effort in the promotion of their political causes. Their rationale is that what is gained at the bargaining table can be taken away from unions through legislation. AFL-CIO's formal political organization which functions at the national, state, community and local union level is the Committee on Political Education (COPE).

PREVAILING WAGE: In 1861, Congress passed a prevailing wage rate law which said in part: "That the hours of labor and the rates of wages of the employees in the navy yards shall conform as nearly as possible with those of private establishments in the immediate vicinity of the respective yards."

PRODUCTIVITY: The measure of efficiency in production. The comparison of resources used in creating goods and services. If the same resources that were used in the past produce more goods and services, productivity has increased.

PROHIBITED PRACTICES: Generally used in public employment to describe unfair labor practices on the part of employer and employee organizations.

READING FORMULA: The procedure with which union recognition was achieved in factories during the 1930s. Rather than being compelled to strike for union recognition, the new Wagner Act provided a method of union representation elections which were conducted by the National Labor Relations Board.

REAL WAGES: Wages expressed in terms of what today's dollar will buy. A common method of determining buying power is through the Consumer Price Index.

REDEMPTIONER: A white emigrant from Europe who paid for his or her voyage to the New World by serving as a servant for a specific period of time. Also known as a freewiller.

RIGHT TO WORK LAWS: The term used by opponents of unions to institute open-shop laws in the state. The expression has nothing to do with guaranteeing anyone the right to a job.

SABOTAGE: From the French word "sabot" or wooden shoe which workers threw into the machines to keep them from working. Workers have been perpetually fearful that new machines would take their jobs away from them and sabotage was one of their early answers to the Industrial Revolution. It was also a part of strike violence where strikers incapacitated machines or buildings in order to shut down production.

SCAB: A worker who refuses to join the union or who works while others are striking. Also known as a "strikebreaker."

SECONDARY BOYCOTT: An effort to disrupt the business of an employer through boycott techniques, even though his own workers are not directly involved in the labor dispute.

SENIORITY: A worker's length of service with an employer. In union contracts, seniority often determines layoffs from work and recalls back to work.

SEPARATION PAY: Payment to a worker who is permanently laid off his job through no fault of his own.

SERVICE FEE: Money, usually the equivalent of union dues, which members of an agency shop bargaining unit pay the union for negotiating and administering the collective bargaining agreement.

SHOP UNION: Established by the Knights of Labor in the 1880s. Shop unions in the factory carried out the rule enforcements of the local assemblies.

SIT-DOWN STRIKE: In June, 1934, Rex Murray, president of the General Tire local in Akron, Ohio, discussed a pending strike with fellow unionists. If they hit the bricks, the police would beat them up. But if they sat down inside the plant and hugged the machines, the police wouldn't use violence. They might hurt the machines! So began the era of the sit-down strikes effectively used by unions like the Rubber Workers and Auto Workers to build the CIO. The sit-down period lasted only through 1937, but it provided labor history with one of its most colorful chapters.

SLOWDOWN: A form of protest where workers deliberately lessen the amount of work for a particular purpose.

SOCIAL UNIONISM: Unions which look beyond immediate objectives to try to reform social conditions and which also consider unionism as a means of appealing to needs of members which are not strictly economic. In addition to fighting for economic gains, social unions have education, health, welfare, artistic, recreation, and citizenship programs to attempt to satisfy needs of members' whole personalities. Labor, social unionists believe, has an obligation to better the general society.

SPEED UP: A word used by workers to describe employer attempts to increase their output without increasing their wages.

STATE SOVEREIGNTY: The idea that the state is king and public employees had no right to make demands on it. In 1949 a New York court said: "To tolerate or recognize any combination of civil service employees of the government as a labor organization or union is not only incompatible with the spirit of democracy but inconsistent with every principle upon which our government is founded."

STOOLPIGEON: A person hired by an employer to infiltrate the union and report on its activities.

STRETCHOUT: A workload increase that does not grant a commensurate pay increase.

STRIKE: A temporary work stoppage by workers to support their demands on an employer. Also called a "turn out" early in the nineteenth century.

SUBCONTRACTING: The practice of employers getting work done by an outside contractor and not by workers in the bargaining unit. Also called "contracting out."

SUPPLEMENTAL UNEMPLOYMENT BENEFITS: A provision in the union contract which provides laid-off workers with benefits in addition to unemployment compensation.

SYMPATHY STRIKE: A strike by persons not directly involved in a labor dispute in order to show solidarity with the original strikers and increase pressure on the employer.

TAFT-HARTLEY: In 1947, Congress passed the Taft-Hartley Act which outlawed the closed shop, jurisdictional strikes, and secondary boycotts. It set up machinery for decertifying unions and allowed the states to pass more stringent legislation against unions such as right-to-work laws. Employers and unions were forbidden to contribute funds out of their treasuries to candidates for federal office, supervision was denied union protection, and the unions seeking the services of the National Labor Relations Board had to file their constitutions, by-laws, and financial statements with the U.S. Department of Labor. Their officers also had to sign a non-communist affidavit.

TAYLORISM: Associated with the principles of "scientific management" advocated by Frederick W. Taylor at the beginning of the twentieth century. Tayor proposed time and motion studies of jobs to enable managers to set standards for more efficient production. Unions argued that Taylorism was the old speed up in modern dress.

TENANT FARMER: When southern plantations were broken up after the Civil War, blacks and poor whites were controlled by landowners through sharecropping. The tenant farmer paid roughly a third of his crop to the landlord, a third for provisions, tools, and other necessities, and he kept whatever was left. Unsuccessful efforts were made in the 1930s to organize tenant farmers by the Southern Tenant Farmers Union. More sustained attempts at farm worker organization are being made today.

UNDERGROUND RAILROAD: A system of clandestine routes toward Canada whereby abolitionists helped fugitive slaves escape to freedom.

UNFAIR LABOR PRACTICES: Defined by the National Labor Relations Act and by the Taft-Hartley Act as practices of discrimination, coercion, and intimidation prohibited to labor and management. Management cannot form company unions or use coercive tactics to discourage union organization. Unions cannot force workers to join organizations not of their own choosing.

UNION LABEL: A stamp or a tag on products to show that the work was done by union labor.

UNION SECURITY: A clause in the contract providing for the union shop, maintenance of membership or the agency shop.

UNION SHOP: A shop where every member of the bargaining unit must become a member of the union after a specified amount of time.

WALKING DELEGATE: A unionist who policed jobs to see that workers were getting fair treatment.

WHITE-COLLAR WORKERS: Workers who have office jobs rather than factory, farm, or construction work.

WOBBLIES: A nickname for members of the Industrial Workers of the World. The origin of the word is unknown.

WORKIES: A nickname for members of the workingmen's associations in the 1820s and '30s.

YELLOW-DOG CONTRACT: A contract a worker was compelled to sign stating that he or she would not join a union. The practice was outlawed in 1932 by the passage of the Norris-LaGuardia Act.

CHRONOLOGY

	POLITICAL HISTORY	THE TECHNOLOGICAL REVOLUTION	LABOR CHRONOLOGY
1617		The wooden plough enters Virginia. Its invention is ascribed to an unknown Egyptian who lived around 2500 B.C.	
1676			Settlers and indentured servants led by Nathaniel Bacon revolt against the aristocratic rule of Virginia's governor, William Berkeley. After initial successes they are destroyed by British troops.
1765			The Sons of Liberty and Sons of Neptune, composed mainly of workers, protest the Stamp Act and other unpopular British actions.
1770			During a scuffle between colonists, many of whom are workers, British troops fire into a crowd killing five people. Patriots use "The Boston Massacre" to whip up opposition to Britain's policies.
1773			The Boston Tea Party sees mechanics and other citizens board ships and toss their tea cargo overboard in protest of the granting of a monopoly of tea imports to the East India Tea Company.
1776	The Declaration of Independence from Great Britain is adopted by Congress.		The colonies declare independence from Britain.
1783	American independence is recognized by the Treaty of Paris.		
1785		Oliver Evans invents the automatic flour mill. Two years later, he patents the high-pressure steam engine.	
1786			Worsening economic conditions after the Revolution bring on a farmers' revolt under Daniel Shays in western Massachusetts. Philadelphia printers strike to protest a wage cut.
1787	The Constitutional Convention is held in Philadelphia. The Northwest Ordinance, which sets up a method whereby people in the Northwest Territory can create states, is passed.		The Northwest Ordinance outlaws slavery in the Northwest Territories. It also provides for public education, freedom of religion, and a method for establishing new states.

1788   The States ratify the Constitution.

The Constitution is ratified. In addition to providing for a strong central government it contains a clause declaring five slaves are the equivalent of three people. Slaves cannot vote but their existence gives southern states more power in Congress.

1789   George Washington is elected President.

The first Congress meets in New York.

The Federal Judiciary Act organizes a Supreme Court, thirteen district courts and three circuit courts. John Jay becomes the first Chief Justice.

1790   The first census shows a population of 3,929,214.

Samuel Slater opens the first American factory at Pawtucket, Rhode Island.

1791   The Bill of Rights is added to the Constitution.

The Bill of Rights is added to the Constitution.

1793   Eli Whitney invents the cotton gin.

The original Fugitive Slave Act is passed. It is now illegal to give aid or comfort to runaway slaves.

1797   Charles Newbold patents the first American cast iron plow, but he is unable to convince farmers to accept it for they say iron poisons the soil.

1798   The Alien and Sedition Acts are passed by the Federalists to try to silence Jeffersonian liberals. In response, Jefferson and Madison draft the Kentucky and Virginia resolutions which argue states could defy laws they deem unconstitutional.

America fights an undeclared naval war with France. Relations with revolutionary France become strained, particularly after the XYZ affair when French Government officials tried to wring bribes from American commissioners.

Political History, cont'd | *The Technological Revolution, cont'd* | *Labor Chronology, cont'd*

1800 Washington, D.C., becomes the nation's capital. Jefferson is the first president to be inaugurated here.

1803 The United States purchases Louisiana from France, doubling the new country's area.

1806 In *Marbury v. Madison*, the Supreme Court establishes the principle of judicial review.

Unions are judged criminal conspiracies at the trial of Philadelphia cordwainers.

1807 Robert Fulton invents the steamboat.

1811 General William Henry Harrison defeats Tecumseh at Tippecanoe.

1812 The United States declares war on Britain. In 1814 the treaty of Ghent ends the conflict, leaving things about the same as they were before the war. However, the young nation shows the British that they can no longer impress its seamen and otherwise violate its national integrity with impunity.

During the War of 1812, Eli Whitney develops the system of interchangeable parts at his gun factory.

1814 In Waltham, Massachusetts, a mill opens that, for the first time, completes in one location all the stages of cotton manufacture.

1819 Spain cedes Florida to the United States.

1820 The Missouri Compromise admits Missouri as a slave state; Maine as a free state.

1822 Denmark Vesey organizes a slave revolt in Charleston, South Carolina. The slaves are betrayed by an informer. Thirty-seven are executed.

1823 The Monroe Doctrine warns Europeans to halt further colonization of Latin America and to cease interfering in its affairs.

1825 Opening of the Erie Canal. The development of inland waterways, along with the building of roads, stimulates the movement of settlers and the opening of markets.

1827   The American labor movement is born when Philadelphia unions band together to promote the ten-hour day.

1828   Construction begins on the Baltimore and Ohio Railroad, the first railroad to carry passengers over rails.

The Workingman's Party is organized in Philadelphia. Similar parties soon spread to other states. They advocate free public education and abolition of imprisonment for debt.

1831   Samuel Colt invents the revolver.

Cyrus McCormick invents the reaper.

Nat Turner leads a slave revolt which kills fifty-seven whites before the slaves are cut down by an overwhelming force.

Abolitionist William Lloyd Garrison begins publishing *The Liberator* as antislavery agitation in the North increases.

1832   South Carolina nullifies the federal tariff. President Jackson considers it an act of rebellion but the issue is soon laid to rest.

The Black Hawk War, precipitated when whites occupied the homes and lead mines of the Sauk and Fox, ends with the massacre of men, women, and children at Bad Axe by the U.S. Army.

Chief Justice Marshall affirms the right of the Cherokees to their land, but President Andrew Jackson ignores the Supreme Court and sends soldiers to forcibly remove the Cherokee along the "Trail of Tears" to Oklahoma.

1834   The formation of the Whig Party under Henry Clay.

Thomas Davenport invents the electric motor.

1835   Seminoles resist being forced out of Florida. The war lasts until 1842.

1836   Mexicans capture the Alamo but are later defeated by Americans at San Jacinto. Texas declares its independence and Sam Houston becomes president of the Republic.

	Political History, cont'd	The Technological Revolution, cont'd	Labor Chronology, cont'd
1837			The Panic of 1837 virtually destroys the burgeoning labor movement.
1839		Charles Goodyear invents the vulcanization process for rubber.	
1840			President Martin Van Buren establishes the ten-hour day for certain federal employees to remove "much inconvenience and dissatisfaction." Washington, D.C., and Philadelphia shipyard workers have earlier struck for the ten-hour day. The Philadelphia workers won.
1842	The Webster-Ashburn Treaty with Great Britain fixes the northeastern boundaries between the U.S. and Canada.		A Massachusetts court backs unions for certain activities in *Commonwealth v. Hunt.*
1844		The first telegram, invented by Samuel Morse in 1832, is successfully transmitted between Washington and Baltimore.	
1845	Texas joins the Union.		
1846	The Mexican War starts when Mexican soldiers cross the Rio Grande. Britain and the U.S. agree on the Oregon boundary.		
1848	The Treaty of Guadalupe Hidalgo ends the Mexican War and recognizes the Rio Grande as the boundary between the two countries. Mexico cedes California and New Mexico to the U.S. for fifteen million dollars.		
1849		Walter Hunt invents the safety pin.	

1850	California is admitted to the Union as a free state. The remainder of formerly Mexican land is divided into Utah and New Mexico.	Cornelius Vanderbilt has control of most of the shipping industry.	Slave trade is abolished in Washington, D.C. A stronger Fugitive Slave Act is passed.
1850s		More than ninety percent of the nation's energy is supplied by wood.	Aided by the westward movement in general and the California gold rush in particular, skilled labor becomes scarce and unions begin to organize. In 1850, in large cities, they win the ten-hour day and wage increases. By the end of the decade several national unions have been founded.
1851		Elisha G. Otis invents the passenger elevator.	
1852			Harriet Beecher Stowe publishes *Uncle Tom's Cabin,* providing momentum to abolitionism.
1853	The Gadsden Purchase results in more Mexican land being included in the United States.		
1854	The Kansas-Nebraska Act, which declares that citizens of the states will decide the slavery question, repeals the Missouri Compromise. Settlers in Kansas battle one another as the slavery issue heats up.		The Kansas-Nebraska Act, which gives the states the right to decide the slavery question, leads to violent clashes particularly in Kansas.
1856	The Republican Party holds its first convention.	The first railroad bridge over the Mississippi is constructed at Davenport, Iowa. The Wabash and Erie canals are completed this year.	
1857	The U.S. Supreme Court's Dred Scott decision rules the Missouri Compromise unconstitutional. The Court holds that a former slave has no liberty even in a free state.		In the Dred Scott case, the Supreme Court states that a black is not entitled to citizenship rights.
1858		First stagecoach from St. Louis west makes coast-to-coast trips possible on public transportation.	
1859	John Brown raids Harper's Ferry, Virginia, to obtain arms for slaves to help them fight for their freedom. He is hanged for treason.	Oil found at Drake's well in Titusville, Pa.	John Brown raids the Harper's Ferry Arsenal. He has planned to arm slaves and precipitate a revolt. Brown is captured and hanged for treason.
1860	Lincoln is elected President and South Carolina secedes from the Union.		

	Political History, cont'd	The Technological Revolution, cont'd	Labor Chronology, cont'd
1861	The Confederacy of Southern States is formed with Jefferson Davis as its president. West Virginia severs ties with Virginia. The nation is thrown into a traumatic Civil War.	Telegraph lines link East to West for the first time.	The Civil War begins. While there are other issues, a major cause is the southern labor problem of slavery.
1862		The battle between two armored warships, the North's "Monitor" and the South's "Merrimac," ushers in the era of steam-powered, iron-plated naval ships. Richard Gatling invents the machine gun.	President Abraham Lincoln issues the Emancipation Proclamation freeing slaves as of January 1, 1863.
1865	Lee surrenders to Grant, ending the Civil War. Lincoln is assassinated.	The first oil pipeline is in operation.	The Civil War ends in victory for the North. The 13th amendment abolishing slavery is ratified.
1866		Cyrus Field is responsible for laying the first successful trans-Atlantic cable.	The National Labor Union is organized by labor and reform groups to advance the cause of labor, social, economic, and political reform.
1867	The Reconstruction Acts are passed in an effort to insure liberty for former slaves. The South is divided into military districts. The U.S. purchases Alaska from Russia.		The Grange is founded to ease the drabness of rural life. It soon becomes a powerful spokesman for farmers who feel victimized by corporations.
1868	President Andrew Johnson is impeached by House but escapes conviction by one vote in the Senate.	Christopher Shoales patents the typewriter.	The fourteenth amendment is ratified. It prohibits the states from denying any person within their jurisdiction "equal protection of the laws."
1869	The fifteenth amendment, which gives blacks the right to vote, is passed.	The transcontinental railroad is completed.	Uriah S. Stephens founds the Noble Order of the Knights of Labor. Men and women of "every craft, creed and color" are accepted for membership.
1870		John D. Rockefeller organizes Standard Oil.	
1871	The exposé of corruption at Tammany Hall eventually sends Boss Tweed to prison. The first Civil Service Commission is created.		

1873   The labor movement loses much of its momentum when a severe depression causes widespread unemployment.

1874   The first electric trolley is in operation.

1875   Barbed wire is marketed.

In the Pennsylvania anthracite region, James McParlan, a Pinkerton agent, exposes the Molly Maguires who have terrorized employers. A number of Mollies are hanged.

1876   The Sioux, under Sitting Bull, defeats troops of General George Custer at Little Big Horn.

Alexander Graham Bell patents the telephone which is shown at the Centennial Exhibition.

1877   The United States celebrates its 100th birthday.

The Reconstruction of the South ends.

Riots spark the hot summer air as railroad workers strike to protest wage cuts. Class war breaks out in a number of cities. Federal troops put down what is taking on the aspects of a general insurrection.

1879   Edison patents the first practical incandescent bulb.

1881   President James A. Garfield is assassinated by a disappointed office seeker. The incident leads to the Civil Service Reform Act of 1883.

1882   White opposition to Chinese labor culminates the Chinese Exclusion Act.

On September 5, the first Labor Day parade takes place in New York City.

White riots and other disturbances against Chinese laborers in California force passage of the Chinese Exclusion Act.

1883   The Pendleton Act replaces political patronage in civil service with the principle of a merit system for hiring and promotions.

1884   The Bureau of Labor is established. It later grows into the U.S. Department of Labor.

1886   Police march on a peaceful rally led by anarchists, at Chicago's Haymarket Square, plunging the eight-hour day and protesting police violence against Mc-Cormick strikers. A bomb explodes killing and wounding police who open fire on the crowd. No one knows who threw the bomb or how many were killed but the incident is used to whip up hysteria against all unions. While some of the anarchist leaders are hanged, others are pardoned by Governor John Peter Altgeld who says the case against them has never been established. Chief losers are the Knights of Labor whose membership peaks at 700,000 this year. The Knights soon plummet out of existence.

On December 8, the American Federation of Labor is founded in Columbus, Ohio. Cigar maker Samuel Gompers becomes its first president. The Federation is organized along craft lines and it takes on a conservative coloration, believing that any hint of radicalism will turn the public against unions.

1889   The Oklahoma land rush opens the Oklahoma Territory for settlement.

A conference between the United States and Latin American nations sets up the Pan-American Union.

1890   Congress passes the Sherman Antitrust Act and a high protective tariff.

1891   The Populist Party is formed to advance the cause of the farmers.

1892

Steelworkers at Carnegie's Homestead plant near Pittsburgh strike against a wage cut. The dispute is marked by a pitched battle between strikers and Pinkerton strikebreakers ensconced in barges. The strikers win the battle but lose the war when the Governor sends in the militia to break the strike.

1893 American business and professional men, backed by U.S. troops, overthrow the Hawaiian Kingdom. Samuel Dole becomes first president of the Republic.

1894 Protesting a wage cut while the company registers twenty-six million dollars in profits, Pullman car workers near Chicago ask Eugene V. Debs to lead their strike. The strike becomes so effective that not a train with a Pullman car on it moves anywhere in the country. The federal government breaks the strike with troops. It also issues an injunction and Debs and other leaders are jailed for refusal to obey it.

Jacob S. Coxey, an Ohio businessman, rallies the unemployed to march on Washington to persuade the government to set up a public works program. The marchers dwindle to several hundred when they reach the capital. They are easily dispersed by the police.

1895 Duryea produces the first gas-powered automobile.

Southern states pass "grandfather clauses," literacy tests, and poll taxes, to deny blacks the vote.

1896 In *Plessy v. Ferguson*, the Supreme Court declares its "separate but equal" doctrine.

1897 First of the nation's subways opens in Boston.

1898 The Spanish American War begins after the Maine explodes in Havana harbor. In the Treaty of Paris, Spain cedes the Philippines, Puerto Rico, and Guam to the U.S. It grants Cuba independence.

The war between U.S. troops and Filipinos begins. It ends when American soldiers use a heavy hand to crush all resistance.

Erdman Act authorizes government mediation in labor disputes involving interstate commerce.

1899 The U.S. participates in the Hague Conference which sets up a permanent center for arbitration of disputes between the nations.

Germany and the United States divide up Samoa.

Hatters of Danbury, Connecticut, declare a boycott against the Loewe Company for refusal to negotiate. The Supreme Court says the boycott restrains commerce under the Sherman Antitrust Act. The homes and bank accounts of the Danbury Hatters are attached to pay the $252,130 fine.

Ninety percent of Pennsylvania's anthracite miners strike against a wage cut and for the abolition of company doctors and company stores. The importation of European immigrants and the occupation of the area by soldiers fails to break the strike. An arbitration commission finally awards strikers the nine-hour day and a modest wage increase but it fails to recognize the union.

Birth of the Industrial Workers of the World which advocates unions running economic institutions. The IWW favors direct action, industrial unionism, and the general strike. The union wins the Lawrence textile strike of 1912. It fades after losing the Seattle General Strike of 1919. Most IWW leadership is jailed in the 1919-20 Palmer Raids.

Coal replaces wood as the chief source of energy.

Elbert Gary, backed by J. P. Morgan money, buys out Carnegie interests and combines other firms to create U.S. Steel.

Wilbur and Orville Wright make their first successful airplane flight at Kittyhawk, North Carolina.

Motion pictures make their first commercial appearance in McKeesport, Pennsylvania.

1900 Hawaii is annexed to the United States.

The Socialist Party is founded under the leadership of Eugene V. Debs.

The United States intervenes in the Chinese Boxer rebellion. The U.S. warns European powers not to dismember China.

1901 President McKinley is assassinated. He is succeeded by Theodore Roosevelt.

1902

1903 Panama revolts against Columbia. American ships help insure the Revolution's success. A treaty between the new nation and the United States gives America the canal zone.

1904 President Roosevelt declares the U.S. has an obligation to maintain order in Latin America.

1905 Roosevelt wins the Nobel Peace Prize for mediating the war between Japan and Russia. Their treaty is signed in Portsmouth, New Hampshire.

1906   A devastating fire, resulting from an earthquake, destroys San Francisco.

1907   Hostility to and discrimination against Japanese by whites in San Francisco lead to a "Gentlemen's Agreement" between the U.S. and Japan whereby no more Japanese would enter the United States.

The "Gentlemen's Agreement" with Japan is the result of racial outbursts against Japanese in San Francisco, primarily because of job competition between whites and Japanese. Japan is forced to restrain its citizens from coming to mainland U.S.A., an insult it never forgets.

1909   Robert E. Peary discovers the North Pole.

Birth of the National Association for the Advancement of Colored People led by W.E.B. DuBois to advance job and other rights of blacks.

1910   Ford begins mass-production automobile industry.

A labor party in Milwaukee cleans up corruption, institutes planning and efficient service in a "City Beautiful" that becomes a national model for excellence in government. Unfortunately, another kind of labor party in San Francisco is so blatantly corrupt that it sours voters on union politicians.

1911   The combine is invented by Benjamin Holt.

One hundred fifty-four workers, mostly young women, die in a fire at the Triangle Waist Company, New York City. Fire escapes end in mid-air, doors are locked. The factory commission which sprang from the tragedy's ashes presses the Legislature into passing the first serious safety laws for working people.

1912   U.S. Marines land in Nicaragua to protect American interests during a rebellion.

The Lloyd-LaFollette Act abolishes presidential gag orders on federal employees which deny them the right to lobby on their own behalf. It also recognizes their right to organize.

1913   The sixteenth amendment, the income tax, is ratified. The Federal Reserve System is established.

U.S. Department of Labor is established.

1914

The U.S. intervenes against Mexican revolutionaries.

The Federal Trade Commission is established.

The Clayton Antitrust Act supplements the Sherman Act.

U.S. Naval forces occupy Vera Cruz, Mexico, after shelling it.

The Panama Canal is opened.

The Panama Canal is completed.

Colorado militia sweeps a strikers' tent colony near Ludlow with machine gun fire and then proceeds to burn tents with people inside them. Thirty-nine men, women, and children are killed. This is the culmination of a twenty-year class war in the Rockies. Following the Ludlow Massacre, miners, wearing red bandanas, rout the militia but President Wilson sends in federal troops to end the war. All those who participate in the massacre are absolved from wrongdoing.

The LaFollette Seamen's Act establishes much-improved working conditions, food and living allow-ances for sailors. It also protects them from human sharks who exploit them while in port.

1915

1916

Expansion of state highways throughout the nation begins with the passage of the Federal Aid Road Act.

Congress passes the Adamson Act which establishes the eight-hour day on interstate railroads.

1917

Congress declares war on Germany.

Congress passes the Espionage Act, the Trading with the Enemy Act, and Selective Service.

The first radio station, WHA, University of Wiscon-sin, Madison, is established. KDKA, Pittsburgh, begins commercial programming in 1920.

1918

Germany surrenders.

The Sedition Act, resulting in mass arrests for those opposing the war, is passed by Congress.

1919

The Boston Police strike is snuffed out by the National Guard. Calvin Coolidge takes credit for breaking it and becomes an instant national celebrity. Congress passes a law making it a misdemeanor for police or firefighters to affiliate with unions.

A bitter and massive strike by steelworkers ends in the union being crushed.

Employers launch the American plan to combat unions.

1920   The 19th amendment gives women the right to vote. Eugene V. Debs, running for President from prison, polls nearly a million votes.

1922   The big powers agree to limit their naval forces.

1923   The Teapot Dome scandals reveal widespread corruption in the Harding Administration.

1925   John Scopes, a Tennessee schoolteacher, is convicted for teaching evolution.

1926   Congress passes the Railway Labor Act which establishing bargaining in the industry.

1927   Lindbergh makes first solo across the Atlantic.

1928   The Kellogg-Briand Pact outlawing war is ratified by the Senate.

1929   The stock market crash throws the nation into a severe depression.

1930   The Hawley-Smoot Tariff Act brings tariffs to their highest level in history.

1932   The Norris-LaGuardia Act restricts injunctions against strikers and outlaws yellow-dog contracts.

Wisconsin passes the nation's first unemployment insurance law.

1933   The first hundred days of Franklin D. Roosevelt's administration brings forth a host of economic recovery legislation.

1934   A violence-laden strike in Minneapolis, the killing and wounding of nearly seventy people, leads to a dramatic teamster victory for over-the-road drivers.

In San Francisco, longshoremen battle police on Rincon Hill and on "Bloody Thursday". Three pro-unionists are killed and 115 strikers and police are wounded. A general strike aids the union cause. The dispute finally goes to arbitration where the union wins benefits and recognition.

1935

New Deal laws enacted include the Wagner Act, the Works Progress Administration, the Resettlement Administration, and the Social Security Act. The Supreme Court, threatened with a "packing" by Roosevelt, responds by okaying the New Deal.

The sit-down strike is born at the General Tire plant in Akron, Ohio.

Congress passes the Wagner Act which establishes the first national labor policy of protecting the right of workers to organize and to elect their representatives for collective bargaining.

The Committee for Industrial Organization, headed by John L. Lewis, is formed within the AFL to advance the cause of industrial unionism.

1936

The first CIO strike, which includes a mile-long picket line, ends in a victory for Akron Goodyear workers.

The Public Contracts Act sets labor standards for government contracts.

1937

Ten CIO unions are expelled from the AFL for "dual unionism."

Auto workers win bargaining rights after a historic sit-down strike at the Flint, Michigan, General Motors plant.

On Memorial Day, Chicago police fire on unarmed steelworkers, killing ten and wounding over a hundred. It is a Pyrrhic victory for employers. By 1941 the union has nearly swept the industry.

Industrial unions found the Congress of Industrial Organizations (CIO).

1938

The Fair Labor Standards Act, which abolished child labor and set a twenty-five-cents-an-hour minimum wage, is passed.

The Fair Labor Standards Act is passed. It sets a minimum wage of twenty-five cents an hour and it outlaws child labor in business under its jurisdiction.

More than forty Hilo, Hawaii, unionists are shot and bayonetted by police as they assemble on a public pier as an act of protest during a ship strike.

1939　The United States pledges its neutrality after war breaks out in Europe.

TV is demonstrated at the New York World's Fair.

1940　Congress passes the Smith Act making it unlawful for anyone to advocate the overthrow of the government or to be a member of any organization advocating such a goal.

1941　The Japanese attack Pearl Harbor. Congress declares war on Japan. Germany and Italy declare war on the United States.

The Office of Production Management, National Defense Mediation Board, and the Office of Price Administration are set up to try to maintain stability in wages and prices.

After the attack on Pearl Harbor, the AFL and the CIO sign a no-strike pledge for the war's duration.

1942　President Roosevelt issues the Japanese Relocation Order which uproots over 100,000 Japanese-Americans and herds them into relocation camps.

The National War Labor Board is established. It issues the "Little Steel Formula" which pegs wage increases to rises in the cost of living.

1943　Italy surrenders to the United States.

First tests of jet planes in the United States. The first self-sustaining nuclear reaction takes place at the University of Chicago.

A Fair Employment Practices Committee is established by the government to try to eliminate discrimination in war industries based on race, creed, or national origin. Women have also entered war industries in droves, and symbols like "Rosie the Riveter" assert they can do the jobs of men in the world of work.

The Smith-Connally Act is passed which authorizes the President to seize plants if necessary to maintain the full war effort. When nine workers strike, the President seizes the mines.

1945　Germany unconditionally surrenders. The United States forces Japan into submission by dropping the atomic bomb on Hiroshima and Nagasaki.
The Potsdam Conference plans the division of Europe among the allied powers.
The United Nations is formed.

The atomic bomb is exploded in Japan.

1946 The Atomic Energy Commission is established under the principle of civilian control.

The Philippines gains independence from the U.S.

1947 General George C. Marshall proposes a plan for the recovery of Europe.

The Truman Doctrine attempts to stop the spread of communism by aid to Greece and Turkey.

1948 President Truman's executive order ends discrimination in the armed forces.

The U.S. airlift counters a Soviet move to blockade West Berlin.

1949 The North Atlantic Treaty Organization is formed.

President Truman's Point Four Program stresses technical assistance to developing nations.

1950 North Korea invades South Korea. The United Nations takes action. The U.S. contributes the lion's share of military support.

Presper Eckert and John Muchly invent the electronic computer.

The transistor is invented by J. Bardeen, W. H. Bratair, and W. Shockley.

Upon the end of the war, a wave of strikes puts four and a half million workers on picket lines.

Walter Reuther rises to national prominence when he asks General Motors to open its books to prove it cannot grant the wage increases the UAW demands. GM refuses and 200,000 auto workers hit the bricks. Meanwhile, Steelworkers settles for eighteen and a half cents after a thirty-day strike. After striking GM for 113 days, the UAW wins also.

Sugar workers strike in Hawaii to establish their union and a lot more besides. Led by the ILWU, the strike is the culmination of a forty-six-year effort to bring social, industrial, and political democracy to the territory outside of Honolulu.

The Taft-Hartley Act is passed over President Truman's veto. It outlaws the closed shop, jurisdictional strikes, and forms of secondary boycotts. It opens the door to state open-shop laws.

New York and Michigan pass laws prohibiting public employees from striking.

The CIO starts expelling unions accused of following the communist line.

1952	The first microwave facilities for transcontinental television are completed.	The Supreme Court declares President Truman's seizure of steel mills during a strike unconstitutional.
1953	The Korean War ends.	The AFL expels the International Longshoremen's Association for corruption.
1954	The U.S. Supreme Court in *Brown v. Board of Education*, Topeka, Kansas, outlaws segregation in the schools. U.S. involvement in Southeast Asia begins with the formation of SEATO and to aid governments in Indo-China.	
1955		The AFL and the CIO merge. George Meany is elected president.
1957	Congress passes the Civil Rights Act in order to secure voting rights for blacks. Governor Orval Faubus calls out the National Guard in an effort to stop school integration at Little Rock, Arkansas. President Eisenhower sends in federal troops to see that the law is obeyed.	The AFL-CIO expels three unions for not meeting its code of ethical practices.
1958	The U.S. launches an earth satellite. The first U.S. earth satellite is launched.	One thousand workers strike the Harriet-Henderson, North Carolina, textile mills. Governor Luther Hodges calls out the National Guard. Textile Workers Regional Director Boyd Payton and other union leaders are found guilty of conspiracy to bomb a mill on the testimony of a single man. The defendants are given prison sentences according to their union rank. The case becomes a national cause célèbre and finally Payton is pardoned by the new governor in 1960.
1959		The Landrum-Griffin Act is passed after the McClellan Committee exposes corruption in several unions. The law issues a bill of rights for union members assuring them freedom of speech and assembly. It requires unions to file financial statements and officers and staff to be bonded.
1960	Oil overcomes coal as leading source of energy.	A landmark strike is conducted by the United Federation of Teachers in New York City for a union

	Political History, cont'd	The Technological Revolution, cont'd	Labor Chronology, cont'd
			representation election to enable teachers to bargain. From this time on public employee unions change their tactics from preoccupation with lobbying to stressing collective bargaining.
1961	An invasion attempt of Cuba fails at the Bay of Pigs.	Alan B. Shepard, Jr. is first American in space.	
1962	President Kennedy convinces the Soviets to dismantle their weapons in Cuba.		President Kennedy's Executive Order 10988 recognizes federal employee unions, including their right to bargain.
1963	President Kennedy is assassinated.		The cause of women workers is aided when Congress passes the Equal Pay Act prohibiting wage discrimination because of sex.
1964	Congress passes the Civil Rights Act which prohibits segregation in public facilities and accommodations.		
1966	The Medicare Plan is established. The War on Poverty gains momentum.		Farm workers, led by Cesar Chavez, join the AFL-CIO and march 300 miles from Delano to Sacramento to dramatize their grievances. The farm workers' boycott of nonunion grapes involves more Americans than any previous effort.
1968	Assassinations of Martin Luther King and Robert Kennedy.		Martin Luther King is assassinated while aiding a strike of Memphis sanitation workers. The bullets that kill King fail to defeat the American Federation of State, County and Municipal Employees strikers whose victory has since been considered a victorious turning point in public employee organization. The Age Discrimination in Employment Act prohibits bias against persons aged forty to sixty-five.
1969	Americans land on the moon.	Neil Armstrong and Edwin Aldrin are the first humans to land on the moon.	

1970   Two hundred ten thousand postal workers strike eight cities, winning a six-percent pay increase.

Hawaii and Pennsylvania pass legislation giving most public employees the right to strike.

The Occupational Safety and Health Act is passed which authorizes the Secretary of Labor to establish health and safety standards and to enforce them.

1971   The twenty-sixth amendment granting voting rights for eighteen-year-olds is ratified.

1972   President Nixon visits China and the Soviet Union.

Watergate burglars are discovered in the Democratic Party's national headquarters.

1973   The Watergate affair captures the political scene.

Vice-President Spiro Agnew resigns under charges of corruption. Gerald R. Ford replaces him.

1974   President Nixon resigns as more revelations of official wrongdoing are exposed.

1975   The South Vietnamese and Cambodian governments fall to insurgents. The U.S. pulls out of Indo-China.

1976   America celebrates its 200th birthday.